Triple Crown

Ted Mahovlich

TRIPLE CROWN

The Marcel Dionne Story

HarperCollins*PublishersLtd*

Triple Crown

© 2004 by Ted Mahovlich. All rights reserved.

Published by HarperCollins Publishers Ltd

No part of this book may be used or reproduced in any manner whatsoever without the prior written permission of the publisher, except in the case of brief quotations embodied in reviews.

First Edition

HarperCollins books may be purchased for educational, business, or sales promotional use through our Special Markets Department.

HarperCollins Publishers Ltd
2 Bloor Street East, 20th Floor
Toronto, Ontario, Canada
M4W 1A8

www.harpercollins.ca

Library and Archives Canada Cataloguing in Publication

Mahovlich, Ted, 1968–
Triple crown : the Marcel Dionne story /
Ted Mahovlich. – 1st ed.

Includes index.
ISBN 0-00-200072-5

1. Dionne, Marcel, 1951– 2. Hockey players –
Canada – Biography I. Title.

GV848.5.D56M33 2004   796.962'092
C2004-904569-5

HC 9 8 7 6 5 4 3 2 1

Printed and bound in the United States
Set in Monotype Plantin

To the Dionne family

Foreword

'M OFTEN ASKED if working for *Hockey Night in Canada* represents the realization of a boyhood dream. The answer is no. My dream was to play. I was an only child who got hooked on hockey in 1964, at the age of four, when my father, Corporal Ron Francis MacLean, was stationed at CFB Hillcrest in Whitehorse, Yukon. Winters were long, snowfalls heavy, but in the arctic air the snow itself had that feathery texture that made shovelling a breeze. From that moment on I played every conceivable variation of hockey until I was seventeen. Once in a while, every ten games or so, the sport was easy. I could see the ice, read plays and skate like the wind. One in ten good nights gets you to midget triple-A.

At eighteen I embarked on my broadcasting career in Red Deer, Alberta. That same year I started refereeing hockey. At twenty-four I auditioned to host the Calgary Flames telecasts. I was hired, but told to put the brakes on using big words. The executive producer called me into his office, pointed his finger at me and said, "For you, MacLean, no words larger than 'marmalade.' We're selling beer here!"

So here I was, a kid who loved to shovel snow and was now evidently selling beer, covering the National Hockey League. Within two years my career took me to *Hockey Night in Canada*, where I was given my winger for a life in hockey, Don Cherry.

The dream was to centre Dionne—I got Donnie. These two are closer than you think.

Although I had worked on telecasts involving Marcel Dionne, related many stories about him and admired him from the professional distance of my job, my first clear memory of Marcel takes us to Glanbrook Arena, near Hamilton, Ontario. I was a Level 5

Ontario Hockey Association referee assigned to handle a junior game between the host Glanbrook Rangers and Chippewa. In the arena lobby, before the game, there was Marcel. He was helping out as a coach for one of the teams. "Look at that guy, always smiling," he said, referring to me. I never forgot that line. In one simple phrase, a Hall of Famer lifted me to that strange place a compliment takes you. Strange? Well, yes, because you're left wondering what you did to deserve it. How is it that such an innocent remark can feel so nice? To tell you the truth, that moment is the reason I'm writing this foreword. The night was great, the game terrific. I felt in control—not of the players, but of the purpose of refereeing. And from Marcel's kindness I realized the purpose of hosting hockey shows. To let the guest be the star. Marcel, that was one of your better assists.

I have since had the chance to skate with Marcel in an alumni Hall of Fame game at the Air Canada Centre in Toronto. I was not having one of those "one in ten" nights. As usual, he was.

Marcel Dionne was fast. Sturdy. A terrific passer, a better stickhandler. It's funny; having spent two decades with Don Cherry, listening to him marvel about Bobby Orr, I am always struck by the one thing that most impressed Bobby's father, Doug Orr, about his son. Late one night, Don called up to Parry Sound to tell Doug he had just watched a television special about Bobby's life. Don said, "I knew he was great, but I didn't know he was *that* great. That was somethink! You sure must be proud." Doug replied, "Yeah, he could sure shoot a puck." Now if you asked a hundred experts what Bobby Orr's greatest attribute was, I doubt that three people would say his shot. But that's how his dad saw it.

Like Orr, Dionne could obviously shoot a puck. But if you ask me for the one trait that set him apart, it's understanding—a special ability to anticipate the play on the ice. But Marcel also had an appreciation of the people and the game *off* the ice. This is where I see the link with Don Cherry. Don has long known that the "love of the game" is overrated in pro hockey. Don speaks his mind. He hates phonies. He is a champion of the underdog. Marcel and

Don were together in the 1976 Canada Cup. You'll read about that team and Marcel's role. Don figures *he* set up Darryl Sittler for the winner . . . it was actually Marcel. But "Grapes" rode the buses for sixteen years, and is street savvy. I see so many of these traits in Marcel. Dionne kicks 'em when they're up. He's hard on the ones in the catbird's seat, and quick to rescue those in the dog-house. Marcel saw it all, long before he hit Hollywood.

In Los Angeles he had two key mentors, Bob Pulford and Pat Quinn. At game six of the 2004 Stanley Cup finals in Calgary, Bob Pulford was a guest of Darryl Sutter. The Flames GM and coach wanted to thank "Pully" for all he had done for him in Chicago. *There's* an understanding.

Pat Quinn, in Dick Irvin's 1993 book *Behind the Bench*, said, "I had Marcel Dionne. Marcel had a reputation as a guy who thought about himself ahead of the team. I found out that was a bad rumour because this guy was as good a team player as I have ever been around."

In Bill Boyd's 1998 book, *Hockey Towns*, he points out that, prior to Marcel Dionne, and Yvan Cournoyer before him, Drum-mondville, Quebec's best athlete was weightlifter Rosaire Smith. Smith was a 1948 Olympian and World Championship bronze medallist.

Dionne, too, was a weightlifter. He carried teams and he lifted spirits. How does a man train for such a life? It all starts with shov-elling. And shovelling. And shovelling . . . nothing but snow.

Dig in.

Ron MacLean
Oakville, Ontario
June 24, 2004

Introduction

"**A**LL YOU'D HEAR about was Marcel Dionne, Marcel Dionne, Marcel Dionne," recalls Hockey Hall of Famer Steve Shutt. "And then we went into St. Catharines and I got on the ice, and I go and get a look at Marcel Dionne. Well, here's this little, wee, short guy and I said, '*That's* Marcel Dionne?' Once I saw him play, then I said, 'Oh, that's Marcel Dionne!

"'But he certainly doesn't look like a hockey player.'"

By appearances, Marcel Dionne might have been described as a person suited to a job of honest labour, a trade in which his considerable strength packed into a smaller frame would effectively serve his industry. At first glance the five-foot, seven-inch man would not seem a likely candidate to succeed in a profession in which size is, more and more, considered an asset, if not a prerequisite. As a result of his proportions, Dionne was questioned, doubted, overlooked and misread. And so, while the nonbelievers dismissed him, he quietly set out to do what his deceptively blessed physique would allow. As the story goes, the names that have achieved what Marcel Dionne has done playing the game of hockey can be counted on one hand. They include Wayne Gretzky, Gordie Howe, Mark Messier, and Ron Francis.

In recalling his first encounter with Dionne, Steve Shutt expressed the common perception that Dionne faced repeatedly throughout his life: how could someone his size be all that? On the heels of that first impression comes the realization that Marcel Dionne *is* the exception to the rule. In fact, there are few rules that do apply to him. He has never been common or conventional, and it's no coincidence that the path he chose to follow wasn't either.

———

Introduction

When Dionne joined the National Hockey League as a player for the Detroit Red Wings in 1971, the league was accommodating a series of expansions. Not only was the league in transition, but the game and business of hockey as a whole were in the midst of a metamorphosis. As politics, economics and geography conspired to shape the new NHL, no player mirrored the making over of the sport better than Marcel Dionne.

Of all the capable and diverse talents in the league, why was he the one to forge the model for the modern era? Simply put, he was the right person for the job. Consider the following qualifications. As a top French-Canadian prospect he had displayed a combination of audacity, fear and courage in leaving his home in Quebec to play Junior A hockey in the province of Ontario. As a young captain of an Original Six team he showed confidence, ambition and wits when he forced his club to trade him, resulting in a favourable outcome for himself and his family. As a shrewd businessman dealing with new-breed owner Jack Kent Cooke, Marcel Dionne had the savvy and foresight to secure the most lucrative player contract in hockey history to that point. In the hockey desert of Los Angeles, as a bona fide superstar, he had the necessary determination, perseverance and discipline to carry an entire franchise for over a decade. As a proud ambassador for the Los Angeles Kings, the National Hockey League and Canada, he supported—and helped bring to prominence—the international game by continually answering the call to compete for his country on the world stage. Unequivocally, Marcel Dionne was *the* modern-day player.

Assessing his contributions on the ice further solidifies the significance of the Dionne legacy. But in doing so, one must also consider that compounding the magnitude of that legacy were the circumstances under which his accomplishments were achieved.

At the peak of his professional career Marcel Dionne was immersed in the culture of Los Angeles, California, in the 1970s. While sex, drugs and rock and roll were undoubtedly accessible throughout North America, in Los Angeles they were a way of life. To a young star on a geographically remote NHL team, the southern California lifestyle was ever present, readily available and easily indulged in. Even for those on the straight and narrow path, Los Angeles was, if nothing else, a playground in the sun that was chock full of distractions, none of which, quite remarkably, hampered the focus of the Los Angeles Kings' top player.

Through his years of dedication to a team with neither a storied past nor a string of championships to speak of, Dionne provided a standard of leadership and professionalism. While many of his colleagues possessed modest skills and contrasting levels of commitment, Marcel Dionne was, game in and game out, relentless in the face of opposition. When the dust had settled he had amassed a phenomenal 731 goals and 1,040 assists in a career that spanned 1,348 games played.

In today's NHL, superstars perform amidst an overextended talent pool in a similarly expansive team pool. As a result, the reality for many players is that the universal dream of competing in and ultimately winning a Stanley Cup final may never be realized. Regrettably, this was the case for Marcel Dionne.

Without that elusive championship, some feel that there is a piece missing in what rightfully stands as a Hall of Fame career. Nevertheless, there is something exceptional about it. If one concedes that very few will ever attain the lofty statistics and multiple championships of a Gretzky, Howe or Messier, then closer to Earth, left behind for the players of the modern era to strive for, there remains a benchmark. Those who aspire to reach it must display and maintain a level of commitment, professionalism, courage and raw talent that few can fathom, let alone verge on. Under conditions that could justly be described as defeating, that benchmark was set by Marcel Dionne.

Chapter One

"**MY DAD**, Gilbert Dionne, was born on a farm," Marcel Dionne says. "Just a little town outside of Drummondville called St. Zéphirin. At the age of fifteen my dad left home to become a lumberjack. My dad is a big man, six foot one, 230 pounds. He was the tallest in the Dionne family, which was a large family of eleven kids—he was the fourth brother."

By the age of thirteen, Gilbert was already used to putting in a long day, having spent his summers on a farm working the horses. Because employment as a farm hand was seasonal, Gilbert sought a full-time job elsewhere, leaving school for the Quebec pulp and paper trade. After a relatively brief stint as a lumberjack, he settled in Drummondville, where he worked at various jobs in the textile industry before commencing a long term of employment in a town called Sorel for Quebec Titanium. He worked for the QT, as it was called, for thirty-five years, all the while residing in Drummondville, some thirty-five miles away. It was in Drummondville that Gilbert would make his life with a girl he dated from his hometown.

"We met in a village called St. Zéphirin," recalls Laurette Dionne. "My family, the Sawyers, had a grocery store there. Gilbert would come to our store from the farm and that's how we met." Laurette laughs, "I was a city girl and he was a farm boy. I remember our first date. We went to a movie and he picked me up in a truck with another couple. So there were four of us and the truck could only seat three across. So I sat on his lap on the way to the theatre."

After two years of dating, the twenty-four-year-old Gilbert and the twenty-three-year-old Laurette took their vows. Like the families they came from, and countless others in the healthy Quebec tradition, Gilbert and Laurette soon began a considerable family of their own. They would have eight children in all. On August 3, 1951, their first baby arrived, Marcel Elphège Dionne. "My uncle had died [early]," explains Gilbert. "He was just over twenty when he drowned. Because Marcel was our first son, I thought it would be nice to name him after my uncle. It was the right thing to do and it was nice for my parents."

Marcel's first lasting childhood memory is of a frightening, yet fortunate, visit to the hospital. "At the age of two or three I had surgery—it was for my appendix. To this day I still remember the hospital and I can see my grandfather coming to get me. I guess I almost died. I must have been in pain, and thank God I had a doctor who was able to diagnose me correctly and knew what the problem was. I can remember that experience vividly. There was a swing at the end of the hallway and I thought that was great, to get to go on the swing."

After his episode with appendicitis, the closest the young Dionne would come to trauma was not getting to the outdoor rink in time to clear the snow before it accumulated to a significant degree. Marcel was in good standing in this regard, due to the closeness of his home to the schoolyard. Marcel describes the benefits of living in the neighbourhood that his parents reside in to this day. "They were called parishes in those days, different sections of the town. We lived in a parish called St. Jean the Baptist. The street was 13th Avenue. Our house was right in front of the school. There were two outdoor rinks right at the front of the schoolyard, and in the summer we played baseball there. I could see everything from our front door—which kids were coming to the park that day, when they'd arrive—so it was easy for me to get there. Once the outdoor rinks were ready and the boards were up it was pickup hockey. As soon as I would see guys out there, it was just automatic—out I went. Then ten guys would show up, fifteen guys, and we would play for hours and hours. And I was always the guy who shovelled the snow because I knew that if the snow wasn't cleared we couldn't play. You learn that there is a proper way to shovel snow. I shovelled more snow than anybody else and I never had a sore back. I still shovel snow today, and I've always enjoyed that."

When the snow wasn't falling, Marcel could be found well past midnight at St. Mary's school, flooding the ice, perfecting the surface for the next day's game. Prior to taking on these duties, he had, as a schoolboy, watched his dad building a rink in their backyard. Gilbert remembers his son's affinity for the game, even as a three-year-old. "The man who delivered the bread would sit on the porch watching Marcel, and he was amazed that he could name all the players from the 1950s—Boom-Boom Geoffrion, Rocket Richard. He liked Gordie Howe, too."

As kids growing up in Drummondville, Marcel and his younger brother Rénald shared a bedroom. Reflecting upon their childhood, Rénald recounts with fondness a frequent nighttime scene that corroborates Marcel's passion for the game. "When we went to bed at night we would often play a game. I would pick a sweater from an NHL team, like, 'Who is number nine for the Boston Bruins?' At that time there were only six teams. So, Marcel would have to name the players. Well, he always had the correct name. Sometimes I didn't know if he was right, so I would look it up in a book and sure enough, there it was. I lost all the time with him."

While Marcel was very close with Rénald off the ice, at the rink he had to look to older boys to provide suitable competition for his accelerated hockey skills. This would create a dilemma for the young Dionne. At the age of eight, he was ready to compete at the peewee level, which was nominally for players between nine and twelve. But with the help of his uncle, Gilles Sawyer, who happened to be a brother-in-law of the coach, Marcel was able to circumvent the age restriction.

"Gilles played a big part," says Dionne. "He was the one that took me to an indoor hockey rink. One day he grabbed me when my father was busy working and he said, 'I've got to get you playing organized hockey.' I had never played organized hockey before. It was always pickup, so I wasn't familiar with the blue line and red line. I was only eight years old and when we arrived I was petrified—started to cry. You know, big suck. I was constantly going offside and guys were yelling at me, 'Watch the frickin' blue line!'

"I was deeply hurt by that. To this day I remember that experience. I didn't know where to go on the ice, and this guy who was our big player was making fun of me. But I thank the coach, and my uncle, for sticking by me. And I remembered that guy who laughed at me, and from that point on it was all over for him. I came back the next year and smoked him. I smoked all of those guys."

If enthusiasm for sports is hereditary, Marcel would certainly have acquired that trait from his mother's side of the family. Within the Sawyer clan there exists a great sporting tradition, and Marcel's uncles were known to be fine athletes. Naturally, Marcel received all the support he could hope for from his mother and grandmother, who would follow him to every game. At the arenas, parents of the opposition often approached Laurette Dionne. Bearing the kind offer of a coffee, their friendly conversation would routinely lead to teasing about the licking her son was about to receive. Without fail, by the end of the game it was Laurette who would have the last laugh. The same people who chatted her up before the game would be conspicuous by their absence immediately afterward. Despite his age and size, Marcel established himself as a commanding force on the ice.

Nowhere in the world is there a stronger passion and appreciation for the game than in the province of Quebec. It therefore might not be surprising that, while being immensely fond of Marcel, Grandma Sawyer's appreciation extended to another boy who played for the nearby town of Victoriaville. A competitive lady, she was always entertained when she saw a young fellow named Gilbert Perreault play; even so, she would curse Perreault when his team came up against her grandson's.

A longtime friend and career foe, Perreault played his way up through the ranks alongside Dionne in a province that nurtured brilliant hockey players by the dozens. "Marcel was phenomenal," he gushes. "He was a superstar at a young age—just amazing to watch. Drummondville had a good team, but Marcel was so much better than the others. He could take the puck, deke everybody on the ice, and then score.

"He was playing for Drummondville and I was playing for Victoriaville, which are about half an hour, forty-five minutes apart. At that time we didn't know each other personally; we were eight years old. And as we grew older it just kept going, always competing against one another. It was the same with Guy Lafleur. We all went to the peewee tournament. I was there with Victoriaville, Drummondville was also at the peewee tournament, and Lafleur was there with Thurso. So that's how we got to know each other. Our names were up there all the time—Quebec City had the peewee tournament, Montreal had the big bantam tournament and Drummondville had the big midget tournament. Year after year we were in these tournaments."

In 1961, at a mere ten years old, Marcel exhibited maturity beyond his years on the ice. The same trait would be visible in school and around the house. "Marcel was a good boy," nods Laurette. "We never had to go to his school because he was in trouble."

Surprisingly, Marcel was a loner of sorts. While he did get along with all the kids in the neighbourhood, Marcel never had a best friend per se. "I guess I didn't have time for really close friends beyond those I played sports with. I didn't have *one* guy that would come to my house. I was so active in sports that I played every sport available to me, in the winter and through the summer—everything was strictly sports. I could see when I went to school that there were buddies with buddies. But I never had a friendship like that as a kid, although my brother Rénald did. He'd have friends come over. I guess there were other reasons, too, why I didn't have that."

While Marcel certainly enjoyed the company of his pals playing sports in the yard, he conscientiously gave his time at home to his family. "It was a two-storey house, a typical Quebec duplex. My dad paid $5,000 for it at the time and we would rent out the upstairs to our cousins. They lived there for several years. This was when my dad was working in Sorel and my mother had a business, a little beauty salon in the front of our house. Upstairs were my cousins—there were four boys and a girl—and we were all around the same age. So as the kids in our family were born— you figure three bedrooms, a small kitchen and the same layout upstairs. . . . Every year as more children came along, the house got smaller and smaller.

"First there was me and then my brother Rénald. Then I got five sisters in a row: Linda, Guylaine, Lorraine, Chantal and Marlène. Then my younger brother Gilbert was born when I turned pro. But in that house my brother and I slept in the same bed. It was common in those days—with the families being so big, there could be four in a bed." In order to relieve the squashing of the flock, the cousins who occupied the second-floor apartment moved out in favour of Laurette's parents, Lawrence and Aurore Sawyer.

Through his adolescent years in Drummondville, before hockey would lead him away from his hometown, Marcel forged a close relationship with his grandparents. "I spent a lot of time with my grandfather and my grandmother because I was the eldest. I was very close to them. They moved in upstairs, so we could go up and down, back and forth to see them. And I would go up to eat or just spend time with them. Sometimes my grandmother would make something special for me—she knew what I liked. There was a special stew called *ragoût de boulet*. I've never seen a stew like that since she passed away. It's chicken with meatballs, all in a gravy, and you would eat it with bread to soak it up. That was my favourite and nobody could make that like she could."

Sharing both their natural bond and agreeable companionship, Marcel took full advantage of his grandparents being close at hand. If Lawrence and Aurore were taking off for the weekend,

Marcel would jump at the chance to join them. This offered Marcel experiences outside of their community. "They would take me on trips; like when they went to Ottawa, they would always bring me along. It was really late in my grandfather's life before he owned his first car. I remember when he got it. It was a Dodge and you had to push buttons to change the gears. Looking back, it's amazing that my dad had a car and for all those years my grandfather walked everywhere—or he used a bike. He was very fit and into sports. He did a lot for sports in our community, and my grandmother was a sports fanatic, too.

"But that trip to Ottawa was like, wow! I went to see the Parliament Buildings and all that stuff. I remember going up in the clock tower and looking down. That was a big deal to me. We had a nice time, nothing extravagant; we didn't go out for a fancy dinner. Our thing was to stop at a little canteen to get hot dogs." Marcel laughs. "I like mine with mustard and onions. Those memories are great, and it just meant a lot that they took me along."

With Marcel's father constantly working days, nights and on weekends, and his mother busy raising children, operating a salon and later a convenience store, there was always ample opportunity to help out around the house. Marcel's place as eldest child in a growing family provided a role that he embraced gladly. "I was ten years old and within a year I was working weekends for the store. We sold beer and groceries. My main responsibility was to deliver the beer. Well, in those days you couldn't sell beer on a Sunday—it was illegal—but we still did."

Laurette enjoyed the businesses she ran from their home. The extra income helped their large family and she loved interacting with her customers, especially those visiting her salon. Gilbert had a different take. "I much preferred the store over the beauty salon, because I couldn't stand the smell of the perms that would stay in the house." Lifting his shirt to reveal a pair of surgery scars that form an X across one side of his abdomen, Gilbert declares, "That stench was likely the cause of my ulcers!"

For Marcel, the family store remains a highlight of his youth. Notably exhilarating was the clandestine business of delivering cases of beer, an activity that was as stimulating as any offered in the playground. While he got a tremendous workout hauling the cases and riding his bicycle, he was also exposed to an eye-opening, uncensored side of life. "I'm eleven years old, I've got my bike, I'd get the call, and off I'd go with a couple of cases. I went everywhere; I had a route. I got to know my regular customers—and believe me, I saw everything. Some of the guys were basically alcoholics, and the places I'd go to in those days were filthy. Many of the customers were on welfare and I would be selling beer to them on a Sunday so they could resell it themselves the same day.

"All the customers knew me and respected me so there were never any problems. But I couldn't see my sons doing what I did at that age. To carry all of that money around in your pocket you had to be very responsible—and mature. I mean, some of the ladies I delivered to would look like they had nothing on. And they didn't care. These were rough houses, if you know what I mean. Who knows what they were doing in those days? Well, I know now.

"I would get so excited come Friday because I just loved the whole routine. The phone would ring—two cases of beer. I'd leave with two cases and return with their empties. My bike had a strong, steel-frame basket that I'd put the cases in, and thick wheels. I had to be careful when I turned, or I would lose a case. Can you imagine?

"So I would do the delivery and come back. Tips? Oh yeah, twenty-five cents, fifty cents. Fifty cents was a lot of money in those days. But I would never keep the money for myself. All of the money I collected I put right in the cash register. If I needed money for something, I would go back to the register and take that amount. But I never needed money in those days because I didn't want for anything. You ate at the house and that was it. We drank water, so we never looked for a pop, which isn't to say we couldn't afford it. So if I went to the movies my mother would give me a dollar. We had everything we needed."

For three years, between the ages of eleven and thirteen, Marcel was ecstatic running his beer route. And the more deliveries the better. Although the store sold bread, cereal and other groceries, suds were the main attraction. "Eventually what happened was that we lived off the groceries in our own store. Ninety percent of what we sold was beer, so whatever bread came in—*we* ate it!" laughs Marcel. "And whatever else we stocked.

"Sure, we sold pop, but nobody really cared about that. In those days you had to apply for a licence to sell beer. People could get bread anywhere, but we were one of the few stores that could sell beer. And when people couldn't buy beer on Sunday, they all knew where to go. At the Dionnes' store they would always get what they came for. And we sold a lot of beer. I mean, we'd have our basement loaded full of cases."

Business boomed until a couple of plainclothes detectives spotted a customer leaving one Sunday afternoon with a case. After receiving a hefty fine for the indiscretion, the store curtailed its policy on Sunday beer sales. "We still sold some," offers Marcel, "but we cut way back. And I'll tell you it was a huge business. Sometimes there were four cars in our driveway."

Outside of the excitement from the store, Marcel's childhood was generally a restful time. Fitting that pace nicely were the many afternoons spent at the family's nearby cottage. "I really enjoyed fishing with my grandfather and uncle. We had a cottage at the time in a little town called St. Clotilde. They knew a couple of good spots and we'd fish from four o'clock to five thirty. Now, every time I go fishing, it always brings back memories. It's an incredible sport for a son and father—and grandfather—to share, because it is time with nature. That was very precious to me."

In the role of older brother, Marcel was a steady mate that Rénald, thirteen months his junior, could look up to. "Marcel was very mature for his age and I always followed his lead. He looked out for me and he always told me to take care of your friends, the people you hang around with."

On one occasion, Rénald took on a neighbourhood adversary. Gilbert Dionne didn't like his sons getting mixed up in violence; however, he admired Marcel's resolve to stick up for his younger brother. "Rénald walked in with a black eye, and it was obvious that he got the worst of it in a tussle. So Marcel announced that he was going after the guy that did it, and he was going to sort him out. Just as Marcel was leaving the door, he turned around and asked his brother, 'Does he hit hard?' And Rénald cautioned, 'No, Marcel, there were two or three guys that jumped me!'"

With that bit of information, Marcel's good sense overcame his revved-up state. "I was really brave leaving the door," Marcel grins, "and suddenly I thought about it—whoa. That's probably why I won the Lady Byng a couple of times. I realized I wasn't *that* tough."

Still, being the protector of his kid brother, the elder Dionne worked up his courage. As he resumed his mission to settle the score, now with recruits in mind, Rénald saw the potential for disaster and opted to come clean about the entire incident. "I was with a friend and we ran into a guy that I didn't really like. It was on the street next to ours and we got into a fight, during which he punched me in the eye. But I couldn't see the damage because it was dark out. When I got home Marcel said, 'Hey, you've got a black eye!' Well, I knew that if my dad thought I was in a fight I'd be in trouble, so I made up a story about getting jumped by a group of guys who lived several blocks away from us. So then Marcel wanted to round up his friends and go after them. Then I realized the whole situation was getting out of control.

"I had lied because I was scared of how my dad might react. That was the biggest lie I ever told. And when I explained to my father what really happened, in front of my riled-up brother, he couldn't stop laughing. But Marcel was ready to go. He didn't want anybody picking on me."

By necessity, children of large families learn to be independent and self-sufficient. Undoubtedly, this was the case with Marcel, who thrived on responsibility. Whether it was minding the store and ringing in the till at age twelve or looking after his younger siblings, Marcel never questioned his familial duty. His strong sense of family has always been a top priority throughout his life. In contemplating this side of himself, Marcel revisits scenes that ultimately shaped and affected his appreciation for the fundamental importance of love—and the ability to show it.

Being close to the Sawyer family, Marcel witnessed hard-living folks who struggled in this regard more than people should. "They came from very painful backgrounds. To this day, I can't say that I've ever seen the Sawyers show one another love. Life was hard work and you did your best, but they never told one another that they loved each other. I guess sometimes you don't have to say it, but it was a very cold way to be. And I was raised on that stuff.

"At the time when I was growing up in Drummondville, being the eldest, I saw certain things going on that are not acceptable to me. There was a lot of drinking, and heavy drinking. My uncles were heavy drinkers and when they got together and drank, brothers would fight, sisters-in-law would fight. I was young, but I knew enough to stand my ground. There was a lack of respect and I didn't like that very much.

"Because we had a beer store, a lot of my relatives, or their friends, or my dad's friends, they would all come over and drink like the beer was free. They would just take it from the fridge, and they drank a lot—believe me, I know. They would sit around and drink the profits the family made during the week. In that respect it was a bad situation. But I still enjoyed being around those older people, and very seldom would I leave. I always listened to their conversations or played games with them. If they were playing cards they would include me. They always made me part of it, and that's why I liked each and every one of them. What hurts me now is that we don't see each other on the same playing field."

After leaving for the NHL and establishing his career, Marcel discovered that the relationships he had with the members of his family had changed over time. While Marcel's relatives enjoyed keeping abreast of his life, he regrets the one-sided nature of that attention. "They all followed my career but I never followed them. I feel sad about that. My aunts and uncles are very important to me, every one of them. I wish I could sit down and tell them how much they have to offer in life. I don't think they realized that. They had a lot to offer, but it's not easy coming from a big family. And now that we are older we see each other less and less."

The demands of the taxing schedule during an NHL season absorb the bulk of a player's time, leaving little for even his immediate family. And when Marcel made it back to Montreal to play the Canadiens, he found that what little time he had for his close friends and family would often be taken up by people he didn't necessarily want to be with. For Marcel, that was as frustrating as it was inevitable. But notwithstanding the past, Marcel has in recent years cherished family reunions for the opportunity to reestablish relationships that he missed out on through his career.

Marcel draws a clear distinction between the characteristics of the two sides of his family. He also believes he owes his success to a balance of inherited traits. "I've always had a strong character. Even when I was eight years old I knew where I fit in. It's in the genes. There is no doubt in my mind that my ability to play sports came from the Sawyer family. But my ability to do the work, make the commitment, to focus—that's from the Dionne side. And the two sides are totally separate. The Sawyers were always jocks and partiers. The Dionnes were from the farm—I mean, raising their children, being home [with them] and out to work by six in the morning takes commitment."

As a teenager, Marcel invested all of his free time in developing his athletic ability. However, to complement the benefits of sport, his father, Gilbert, wanted to ensure that his sons had a well-rounded upbringing. One summer, rather than have them continue working at the family store, he arranged for Marcel and Rénald to work on his parents' dairy farm. Even though Gilbert had not chosen a life on the farm for himself, he certainly understood the value of it and felt the education would serve his boys well.

"My brother and I spent a summer on the farm," Marcel beams, "with Grandma and Grandpa Dionne. That was an incredible summer. I was around eleven years old. We would get up early, six o'clock in the morning, and the first thing we had to do was bring in the cows to be milked. Within a couple of hours they would leave, and we would jump on the tractor. The hay was already cut. They let it dry and we would scoop it up with a machine and take it back to the barn. That was a lot of fun. I really enjoyed that summer.

"We lived on the farm with our grandparents and my Uncle Yvon, who was my dad's brother and the baby of the Dionne family. They treated us great. If anybody doesn't know about breakfast on the farm, man, do you eat well. Grandma made the breakfast; it was pancakes, sausage—oatmeal was popular, too. And it wasn't done on an electric stove; it was done on a wood stove. Glass of milk and you were ready to go.

"That was a tremendous experience which I think is really important. And I took my own kids to the farm to show them that side of life. Every person should have that opportunity, to go to a farm and see those animals. It's incredible. Nowadays the operation of the business is more sophisticated, like how they milk the cows. But if you love animals, it's an experience you shouldn't miss.

"To me, a farmer's life is what it's all about. A farmer never throws anything away. There's always a reason to keep something because it will get used later on. Nothing gets wasted. And there is always work to be done. Fixing equipment, repairing fences, it never stops. Whether you like it or not, those cows have to get milked. And the cows become accustomed to you and the routine. When the cows come into the pen, they know where to go.

"What I learned was that the money they had left over was just enough for them to live on. All of my uncles made their money when they sold their farms. Prior to that, they would kill cattle and have beef in the freezer all winter. They also had pigs and chickens, fifty or sixty of them, strictly for consumption. In the morning you would collect all the eggs. And they had huge gardens. It was a self-sufficient life."

A lasting memory of Marcel's father comes to mind. "We had our little store, but that wasn't enough for the family to live on, so we depended on the salary my father brought home in addition to that. One year the QT workers went on strike, but my dad didn't agree with what the union was demanding. He felt the strike was wrong. But to get his allowance he had to go on the picket line, and only then would he receive money to help us get by. Well, he never did join the picket line, and therefore had no income. So my dad said, 'Okay, Marcel, we're going to go pick up potatoes.' I said, 'What do you mean, pick up potatoes?' He said, 'From the potato field. One at a time and put them in a bag—a potato sack.' I worked beside my dad, and I watched that man—six foot one, 230 pounds—I watched him on his knees, because he refused to go on that picket line for what he knew was wrong. He did that for his family so we could survive. These are the types of things you look back at and say, 'Holy shit, I can't believe he did that.'"

―――――――――

With a sound upbringing and a tremendous ability in the sport he loved, it was clear that Marcel had a bright future. Having turned fifteen, Dionne was well on his way to becoming a top NHL prospect. Even as early as age twelve he had received a letter from the Montreal Canadiens organization informing him that they were keeping an eye on him and were pleased with his progress. Now that he was of age to enter the junior ranks, the time had come for Marcel to make his first move from home. "After I finished playing peewee, bantam and midget, there was a Quebec major junior franchise in Drummondville that was a possible next

step for me. That club was sponsored by the New York Rangers—
Emile Francis and company. Basically they approached me when
I was fifteen and I signed on with them. I went to their training
camp and they decided to send me to their affiliate Junior B club
in Montreal. I thought if I played one year there, then I could
come back and play the following year in Drummondville."

The move to Montreal was another positive learning experience, one made easy for Marcel in large part by his aunt and
uncle, Micheline and Bertrand Cloutier. Being great hockey fans,
and more importantly family, Marcel was a welcome addition to
their home. "My uncle in Montreal was a contractor; he laid
asphalt. That was another convenient factor in the equation
because I got to work with him during the summer. And sometimes I would commute home to Drummondville on the weekends. To be able to live with them was a great opportunity and
quite helpful to me. I had never lived away from Drummondville
before, so when I walked into their house, which was a very simple
house, it felt just like home."

When the season commenced for the Montreal East Rangers,
Marcel found his older teammates similarly considerate in his
transition to junior hockey. "When you're fifteen playing with
twenty-year-olds, the age gap is defined by significantly different
mentalities. My teammates were drinking, having sex with girls,
and I wasn't into those things yet. So on the one hand you were in
awe of these big guys, yet at the same time they really looked after
me. In essence, they encouraged me to play hockey and allowed
me to be a boy. It was an exciting time, going to different towns
to play, living away from home. I was just really happy to be with
the team."

As much as Marcel was pleased to feel included on the team,
the Montreal East Rangers were equally glad to have him. The
1966–67 season culminated in a most satisfying fashion. "We won
everything that year. I won the scoring title [with 71 points in 24
games], and then we went to the finals against Flower [Guy

Lafleur]. We killed them," Marcel chortles, "just crushed them."

Lafleur had yet to emerge as the force that would match up against Dionne; it wouldn't be long before that rivalry would commence.

Chapter Two

THE SEASON Marcel Dionne invested with the Montreal East Rangers was beneficial beyond his expectations, providing him with a threefold education: in school, on the ice and on the road. As a player, Marcel furthered his trend of dominating despite his age and size. Having proven himself in Junior B, Marcel was now set for a triumphant return to his hometown—and a spot on the Junior A roster.

To play for the Drummondville Rangers was something Marcel had aspired to, and he expected the convenience and circumstances of the home locale to work in his favour. But Marcel would turn out to be ill prepared for the situation that unfolded. "I think what happened to me happens to a lot of players," he stresses passionately. "When I was sixteen, I was playing hockey in my hometown. In that environment, because of the pressure I was under, because I was the local boy being scrutinized every day, it got to the point where, for the first time in my life, I felt trapped, incapacitated. I was unable to perform on the ice. During a game—I remember that it was the third period—I got up and left. I went to the dressing room, took off my equipment and thought to myself, 'That's it. I'm done. I've had enough and I want to do something else.'"

From the beginning of the season, a combination of pressures had been building inside Dionne, and Marcel was not accustomed to dealing with them. While Laurette and Gilbert never put pressure on their son to play, they could do little to offset the extended family that, consciously or not, Marcel felt compelled to live up to. "A big part of my difficulty was that I had this big family. I had uncles that were tremendous athletes in their day. Having everybody in the family around was like a constant reminder of what was going on in my life. If I didn't get enough ice time in a game it would be, 'How come you're not playing?' Or I'd hear, 'You're better than that guy.'"

While the intent was good-natured family support, the cumulative effect of dozens of hometown relatives' analyses created a heavy burden. Then there were all the neighbourhood friends at school chipping in their two cents' worth. "Geez, I'd go to school and all the guys would come on to you. And they would say things I didn't appreciate or need to hear. Derogatory comments about other teammates, just because they weren't local guys. Well, I liked all the guys on my team, but it felt like people were trying to turn me against them. At that age especially, it wasn't a positive message. Then I would go home after a game and I was the main attraction. People would be in the house arguing about who was the better player on the team—typical hockey talk."

While crises are often eased by the passage of time, Marcel required a more immediate solution for the struggles that he was contending with, on *and* off the ice. After a brief cooling-off period, matters were smoothed out with the coach and organization so that he was able to return to the team after his walkout. Ironically, in his hometown, amongst his teammates, Marcel felt like the outsider. Among other insights, he came to understand why life had been a lot easier the previous season in Montreal. Anonymity in day-to-day life and being in the same shoes as one's teammates were ideal conditions, and they were unattainable for Marcel Dionne in Drummondville.

With a better feeling for his trying situation, Marcel worked through the frustration and he played with even greater confidence. "I want people to know that I struggled with this so when it happens to other players today, in the NHL or elsewhere, they can see it's the same thing I went through. You have to be patient in playing through your rough patches. But I was immature at that time. When people said, 'You've got next year,' I didn't want to hear that. I wanted everything to be corrected immediately, because I knew what I was capable of. I wanted to be told how to remedy the situation. I'd say, 'Tell me, I want to do it now!'"

A solution would present itself in the summer after his season in Drummondville. "Fred Muller from St. Catharines called our house," Laurette recalls. Concerned for her son and his predicament, she was relieved when the call came, despite the fact that her French mother tongue prevented her from taking it herself. "Luckily my brother, Marcel Sawyer, who was bilingual, just happened to be visiting. So he was able to talk with Fred. At that point we made contact and plans for [team representatives] to come to talk with us."

Marcel remembers: "My mom and dad told me that a team from the Ontario league had called when I was in school. Well, my heart started pumping a hundred miles an hour. I had been to see the Montreal Junior Canadiens play in the Ontario league; they had the likes of Pierre Bouchard, Réjean Houle, Marc Tardif, Gilbert Perreault—the whole company. I was in awe. After that I came back and talked to some of my teammates about playing in Drummondville; we concluded that the Ontario Hockey Association was the place to go. So, when the call came, that's what I had been thinking."

Furthering Marcel's desire to leave home were the advantages of being in new surroundings. Along with the sheer thrill of uncharted waters, there was the opportunity to learn English should he relocate to Ontario. "I knew if I was going to pursue my career in hockey that English was going to become part of it. We received the phone call from the St. Catharines Black Hawks, and the Montreal Junior Canadiens were also interested; however, having played there when I was fifteen I knew that Montreal was too close for the change of scene that I wanted. So, St. Catharines came and had a meeting with us in Drummondville. The gentlemen who met with us were Fred Muller, the owner of the St. Catharines Black Hawks, and Johnny Choice. Johnny Choice was a scout for the Chicago Black Hawks. They came and we used my Uncle Marcel as an interpreter.

"At the meeting I told Fred Muller that it was going to be very difficult for me to leave Drummondville. Not for *me* to leave, but for him to get the team to let me go. And I told him that I was looking for a change."

Jack Gatecliff, a sportswriter based in St. Catharine's, describes the dilemma that Fred Muller had to sort out. "I was pretty close to the team at that time. I knew the owner and I did every road trip with the team, covering them for the St. Catharines *Standard.* So I followed them very closely. Before Fred Muller could sign Marcel Dionne, he had to get a branch-to-branch transfer from Quebec to Ontario, which Fred had a difficult time doing. The branch-to-branch transfer allowed players to jump leagues. They've had different rules over the years, but at that time you couldn't transfer anybody from one of the three [major junior] leagues to another without this provision."

Cognizant of the position the Drummondville Rangers were in, Marcel anticipated a backlash. "St. Catharines wanted to make a deal, and they said it was going to be a fair deal that would benefit both teams. But we had won the league championship my first year with the Junior A Rangers in Drummondville, and then lost the provincial title to Verdun. Now, all of a sudden, the Rangers realized they were losing their hometown boy—and more than that, they were building their franchise and it was their star player that was leaving."

Because a marquee player represented fans in the seats and money in the coffers, the departure of Marcel Dionne from Drummondville was, not surprisingly, no easy feat. Although Marcel wanted to move without inconveniencing his family, Muller had no other course but to get the Dionnes jumping through hoops to make it happen. Marcel recalls the soap opera his family went through to allow their son a clean break and a fresh start in southern Ontario. "In order to get the transfer, we were told that the family was going to have to move to St. Catharines. So, my mom agreed to do just that, while my dad was still working in Sorel.

Well, the bad blood flowed in the papers with all kinds of speculation. It went so far as to say that my mom was divorcing my dad.

"My mom had moved to St. Catharines and had been living there for three months with two of my sisters and I. The idea was to pressure the powers that be into allowing the branch-to-branch transfer on the basis that my family appeared to be residing there. Still, Drummondville didn't want to make a deal. I guess the CHA [Canadian amateur hockey association] voted on it and the vote ended up three to two in my favour. Gordon Dukes was the president then. I think the fix was in because there was no reason for me to leave Drummondville—I mean, c'mon.

"The team had rented us a house in St. Catharines and my dad came down a couple of times. We lived there with my mom until they granted the transfer, at which point the family went back to Drummondville. I think I missed the first four or five games of that season. After that my brother came to stay with me in St. Catharines and the two of us moved into a boarding house."

Despite having snubbed the Drummondville Rangers (who clearly got the short end of the stick—St. Catharines sent them a couple of dispensable players) Marcel knew immediately that what his family and Fred Muller went through was worth it. Not only was the claustrophobic home scenario eliminated, but the hockey mindset that Marcel was looking for existed in the St. Catharines organization—and the community—in spades. "I went to camp and I was really motivated. Suddenly everything was new to me. I didn't speak any English—maybe a little bit—but now the environment was really exciting.

"Right away I could feel this electricity running through me. When I walked into the arena there were pictures hanging of Bobby Hull, Dennis Hull, Pit Martin, Stan Mikita—players that went on to play in the NHL. Then I learned about the Cullen brothers, who were very successful there, and the fact that the Chicago Black Hawks' farm team had their training camp there. All of these elements provided me with a guideline. I said to myself, 'Those guys made it, and they played their junior here.' In Drummondville, I had nothing to go by because the franchise was still in its infancy.

"In St. Catharines, now there was some history for me. I could feel the tradition there—wow! And Fred Muller backed me from the time I arrived. He took me aside and said, 'Bobby Hull was a little taller than you and more muscular, but I guarantee you, you are every bit as good, and possibly even better than Bobby.' I didn't believe him, but he knew. He could see what I had in me. I owe that man a lot because of the confidence he showed in me. From that point on I was committed, and I never let him down."

Having finished seventh, eighth, fifth and sixth in the years before Marcel's arrival, the Black Hawks were in a rebuilding phase; Muller was determined to restore the tradition of success he inherited when he bought the Black Hawks, which explains the considerable lengths he went to to procure Marcel Dionne. Bill Bird, who cut his teeth as a sportscaster covering the Black Hawks, recalled the moves Muller was making to return his team to a position of prominence in the OHA: "There were a lot of unspectacular players in St. Catharines before Marcel arrived. Fred was the entrepreneur, so it was really something that he managed to get Marcel out of Drummondville. That very same year he was looking to get Guy Lafleur as well. Can you imagine if he had gotten those two? That's a hell of a story, but it never came to pass."

Excited about the opportunities the Ontario Hockey Association promised, the Dionnes were happy to pay a visit to Thurso, Quebec, on behalf of the Black Hawks, to determine the likelihood of swaying the Lafleurs to St. Catharines. Marcel gave his pitch, only to find that Guy was quite happy to stay in Quebec. "We went to meet Guy's parents to tell them about the great possibilities that playing in Ontario might offer, that Guy and I would play together. But Guy's mother had already met with the Montreal [Junior] Canadiens, and they didn't get him, either. He could have gone to the Montreal Junior Canadiens and he didn't!" Needless to say, the Quebec Junior Aces (who became the Remparts a year later) scored as great a coup in winning Guy Lafleur as the Black Hawks had done in securing Marcel Dionne.

Fred Muller was banking on his young French-Canadian star to turn the team's fortunes around, and in short order that's precisely what Dionne did. Even before he was cleared to play, Dionne showed signs of what was to come.

"I remember the first day of training camp," Bill Bird says. "Actually, I don't know if training camp had even started yet, but Marcel had come into town. He was on the ice with some of the veteran players on the team, and here's this sixteen-year-old kid from Drummondville and they can't take the puck off him. This is before practice even starts. You watched him and it was like, wow, this guy is pretty special.

"He's probably the only guy that I ever saw, certainly in junior, who scored a goal with his team short-handed two men. He did it against Kitchener. Marcel just took it and went from one end to the other. He had the puck in his own zone, and obviously Kitchener was crowding. Marcel just went through everybody, down the ice and stuck it in. And the crowd went crazy. At that point people already knew, but it just put an exclamation point on what kind of special guy this fellow is."

Bird had supported the St. Catharines teams as a youngster— first the Tee Pees and then the Black Hawks—through their highs and lows, so his recollections of the turnaround Dionne initiated are as valid as any. "I had been around as a kid, and I watched in '53–'54 when the St. Catharines Tee Pees won the Memorial Cup. And I watched Fred Stanfield, the two Hulls, Mikita—and those guys were special, too, but there were so many of them back then. After that there was kind of a drought. Kenny Hodge left in '65, and he was sort of the last big name before the situation became pretty fallow. And it remained that way over the next few years. When Marcel came in, that's when the crowds got bigger."

Jack Gatecliff's memories of Dionne's first year in St. Catharines echo Bird's take on the team's resurgence. "He practically brought the team back on his own. It was unbelievable. It was 1968 when Marcel came to St. Catharines, and on the previous year's team, the '67–'68 Black Hawks, the only player that went on to make it in the NHL was Jerry Korab. During that season, the year before Marcel came, Victor 'Skeeter' Teal led the team with 63 points. Well, here comes Dionne the following year, and in his first season he scored exactly 100 points. And that brought all the fans back."

The team's approach with Dionne was simple: just let him have the puck and watch him go to work. There was no denying that Marcel made things happen on the ice; nevertheless, for some of his teammates, having to take a back seat to Dionne was hard to swallow at the time.

"I was a centreman," recalls Skeeter Teal. "When Marce arrived I became the right winger on his line. We were told that Marcel was the up-and-coming star, that type of thing. Well, I had led the team in scoring the year before, but I was told to get the puck to Marcel." Teal snickers. "So it burned me a little bit, but he could handle the puck, and as soon as he got the chance he'd score. You can't take that away from him."

As a hockey player, the transition from Quebec to Ontario was seamless for Dionne. Always seeking out the next challenge, constantly looking to better himself, Marcel had once again ascended to the top. In addition to making his mark on St. Catharines hockey history, Dionne pursued his other personal goal of learning the English language.

In his first few months, he gradually took in what he could at the English-speaking high school his teammates attended. After finding total immersion to be overwhelming, Marcel transferred to a bilingual school in the nearby community of Welland. What Marcel sacrificed in the commute was more than made up for in comprehension of his classes, while his command of English improved steadily.

Through the early going, learning a new language and its subtleties had its moments for Marcel. Brian McKenzie, a close friend to the Dionne family and teammate of Marcel's for each of his three seasons with the Black Hawks, offers a snapshot from that period of adjustment: "Marcel was always a leader on our team. He led by example. You've got to remember, when I first met Marcel, he couldn't speak any English, and we used to have a lot of fun with it. When he came to our school, we'd see him in the hallway and say, 'Hi, Marcel,' and he would just nod his head. Can you imagine how tough that must have been, being in school and not being able to speak the language?

"One of the funniest things I can remember . . . I was sitting beside him on our team bus at the time—and keep in mind that Marcel could barely speak English. We were returning home from a game and we had this bus driver named Charlie. He drove our team on all the road trips, and these guys who drove the hockey teams were good drivers. This one night we were coming home from either the Soo or North Bay and we're in this terrible snow-storm. I just remember the road being really slippery, the snow was coming down, and we came up behind this big tanker truck. All of a sudden it's pitch black and Charlie pulls out to pass. I can still hear Marcel, terrified, screaming in his French accent, 'NO TIME, CHARLIE! NO TIME!' That's all he could say: 'JESUS CHRIST, CHARLIE, NO TIME!'" Once McKenzie's hysterical laughter dies down, he finishes empatheti-cally, "He was just learning then. But he was very inquisitive, and that's how he learned to speak the language."

For the most part, Marcel found his teammates to be support-ive after the requisite introduction to locker-room vernacular. "The first thing that they want you to do is learn to swear, which is typical of guys. Well, I could play along to a certain point but I was never really a follower. So I would do the gig until I just had enough. But the guys knew where I stood, you know, when some-one would call you a Pepsi or a frog and all that stuff. Well, I'll tell you something, if somebody called me that I would let it go, like if it was part of a joke. However, there came a point when they knew, you call me Marce or Marcel. 'Frog' I could take for a while. But they got the picture because I showed self-respect. And the guys were very good. My teammates never really called me those things. My name is Marcel, regardless of the language I speak. Again, we had a character team and a good coach. I was fortunate. They never considered me to be, or treated me as, an import."

The extent to which Fred Muller and the St. Catharines Black Hawks wanted Marcel to feel entirely welcome during his first year was reflected in the midseason acquisition of Guy Delparte from the London Knights. How the bilingual Delparte felt about his brief assignment to an expanded version of special teams is another matter.

"This guy saved me," praises Dionne. "I just followed him around everywhere. Guy was a well-built defenceman, big and strong. You need somebody to rely on and to help you out. He was very important to me. That must have bugged the shit out of him—and they went and traded him.

"Because I didn't speak English, I was incessantly turning to Guy asking, 'What did he say? What's that word?'" Marcel laughs. "He told me to shut up a lot. But he was fun, a really good guy and he respected me. I enjoyed his company. I'll tell you, though, during those first few months, wherever he went, I went with him. I wouldn't leave him alone. It was Guy who showed me how to go about learning English. You have to read a lot, get a newspaper and just read. Watching television helps, too, and eventually you pick it up."

After the departure of Guy Delparte, Marcel had the opportunity to assist his brother Rénald in a similar fashion. The circumstances that brought Rénald to St. Catharines had taken root the previous year, when he decided to take a year off from playing hockey. After the break, at the Drummondville team's request, Rénald tried to re-enlist in his former midget league. When the league president moved to deny his application, questioning his commitment to the sport, Marcel wasted no time in sussing out options for his brother.

"Marcel spoke to the owner of the Black Hawks, Mr. Fred Muller, who told Marcel, 'If your brother would like to come to St. Catharines, that's all right with me.'" Rénald says. "I didn't want to fight with those people at home—who, by the way, had no right to prevent me from playing. Those were English people in charge of minor hockey in Drummondville at that time. It was my feeling that they were jealous of Marcel. So I found it ironic that after I left Drummondville, who took care of me? English people in Ontario. And they were very good to us!"

Whether or not Rénald was the victim of a lasting grudge spawned by his brother's decision to leave Drummondville is debatable. Nevertheless, the situation played out quite favourably for the Dionne boys. Rénald arrived just prior to the end of his family's brief sojourn in St. Catharines, then stayed on with Marcel, who in turn helped him get along with his limited English. While the brothers boarded together for the remainder of their time in St. Catharines, Rénald also got to play hockey, at the midget level in his first year and then for the Junior B Falcons for the next two seasons.

During his midget season, Rénald had the good fortune to meet a congenial fellow at the rink. Unbeknownst to him, this boy happened to have a beautiful sister. "I was skating around during the warmup before a game when I heard someone calling my name. 'Hey, Rénald, how old are you?' The voice was speaking in French and I thought, 'Hey, someone here speaks French.' So I skated over and told him my age, and after the game he was waiting for me. He introduced himself as Gino. I thought that was an odd name for a French person, so I asked if he was Italian. He said, 'No, I'm French-Canadian. My name is Jeanot but they call me Gino.'

"Well, my name is Rénald, but like Gino I discovered that English people had difficulty pronouncing my name correctly. So Gino explained the solution for his name and suggested calling me Ron instead of Rénald, and Ron stuck.

"So he invited me to his home for dinner, where he introduced me to his sister Carol. At dinner I talked with Carol and found that she, too, was a lot of fun. When I got home I told Marcel that I met a guy who doesn't live far from us and his family goes to all the Black Hawks games. I also told him about Carol and thought that she'd be a nice girlfriend."

While Rénald was thinking of getting to know Carol better, Marcel met another friendly hockey fan who coincidentally spoke to him in French. Her name was Dolores Gaudet. "I was on my way to a game, and I remember it was raining so I was running to the rink. A lady stopped me and talked to me in French; it was Carol's mother. She had recognized me because she was a big hockey fan. We just chatted briefly on that occasion."

Dolores had three children—along with Jeanot and Carol there was Gaston, the eldest of the three. The family had moved from Rouyn-Noranda, Quebec, to St. Catharines when Carol was nine, after their father passed away. Always a great hockey fan, Carol's mother faithfully attended the Junior A games in St. Catharines. Like the rest of the community, Dolores was thoroughly awestruck by the skill of the new recruit from Drummondville. Confirming the hype that her daughter was hearing around town, Dolores insisted, "Wait until you see this new kid from Quebec, he's unbelievable!"

Still interested in pursuing Carol, Ron accompanied Gino to a basketball game that Carol was playing in for her high school. Impressed by this active and spirited girl, he was certain that his interest in her was well founded. On the walk home from the game, he asked Gino and Carol if they would like to stop by his house. If Marcel was home, he could then introduce them to his brother. Although Carol graciously accepted the invitation, she had reservations about the highly touted hockey star. "To be honest, my first impression of Marcel was that he must have had a swelled head. All of the clippings I read in the newspaper talked about him like he was a Rocket Richard, and he hadn't even played a game yet. So we stopped at Rénald's house and Marcel came out. And that was the first time we met. Ron introduced us and we said hello and talked. It's funny, because although my mom had season's tickets, I couldn't care less about hockey."

Rénald's account of the meeting is a bit more detailed. "She was so nervous meeting Marcel. When Gino, Carol and I left Marcel, and we continued down the street, Carol started to scream. I thought she was crying, so I asked her, 'What's wrong?' She said, 'I'm so nervous I pissed my pants!' Gino and I started laughing, and Carol was laughing, too. Although, looking back at the situation, I don't know why I was laughing—I wanted her to be *my* girl-friend. After that, it was all Marcel. I didn't even get the chance to kiss her."

Despite Carol's indifference to hockey, after meeting Marcel she was intrigued by his personality and attracted to the person behind the player. And so, when Marcel inquired about her plans for the Black Hawks' next game, she welcomed his offer of a pair of tickets that he left for her at the gate. After the game, they went to a diner across from the rink. From that first date, they hit it off, completely enjoying one another's company.

Carol was looking forward to their next meeting, although she would be surprised by a coincidence that brought it about. "The first time Marcel came to my house it was because my mom had invited him to dinner. I saw him in our house and I said, 'What are *you* doing here?' " Being considerate to Marcel, a French-Canadian new to the community and neighbourhood, Dolores had extended a dinner invitation that he happily accepted. The fact that Carol lived at the same address made the evening all that more enticing. Marcel recalled, "I went to her house and I knew she was going to be my wife."

With a joyful and lasting marriage to back up his bold claim, one can't argue with Marcel's certainty. However, there was more to the evolution that spawned the partnership which Marcel and Carol celebrate to this day.

"I thought Carol's mom played a big role in our being together," affirms Dionne. "She was very personable and very friendly. Then I met Carol's brothers, and they were good guys. But what happened was, I would stop by their house after practices and say hello because they were on my way home from the rink. Then Carol started coming to my games and I would take her home after."

Coming from a strict household, Carol's relationship with Marcel provided a liberation she had only dreamed of. "I had a very early curfew. When I met Marcel he was my saviour, believe me," Carol sighs. "I was seventeen and I had a curfew of nine o'clock. My mother sheltered me because I was her only girl and my father had passed away years before. When Marcel came along, she trusted him so much; it was like she trusted him with her life. And I'm thinking, 'Yeah, sure.' Maybe it was because he spoke French and he was a nice guy that she liked him so much. So I told my mother, 'Once I tell him how early my curfew is, he's not going to come around anymore.' She said, 'Okay, fine.' Then she calculated how long the hockey game would take—they played on Sunday evenings. After they showered it would be 11 p.m., so she said, 'If you can be home by 11:30 or midnight that would be great.' And Marcel would say, 'Don't worry, Mrs. Gaudet, she'll be home on time.' And he never missed a curfew."

Getting into the good books at the Gaudet house was a shrewd move for a young man away from home. Not that Marcel had any bad intentions, but Carol certainly remembers how good he had it. "My mom loved to cook and bake. Even now, she still bakes and he'll eat any dessert that's put in front of him. After practice he used to stop by. I think we even started doing his laundry." Carol jokes, "Maybe that's why he liked me, because I would do his laundry." The jab at Marcel's housekeeping sparks an exchange. Fairly certain that he didn't do his own laundry, Marcel falls back on his billet.

Marcel: "Ethel did my laundry. I never brought my laundry to your house."

Carol: "Marcel, I remember. *I* did your laundry. Maybe not for the entire year, but I remember doing laundry for you. Yes, I did, Marcel!"

Marcel: "You did?"

Carol: "Yes, I did, Marcel—Jesus!"

Marcel: "I don't remember that. Well, I'll tell you right now, this is not going in the book."

At the conclusion of the Black Hawks' first season with Marcel Dionne, the team embarked on a commendable playoff run that was halted in the finals by the Montreal Junior Canadiens powerhouse. Once again, continuing their childhood tradition, Dionne faced Gilbert Perreault in the postseason showdown.

Perreault's path to the NHL was similar to the one Dionne travelled, albeit with a superior supporting cast. "The first year I played junior I played in the Quebec league," he says. "Like Marcel, who played one year in Drummondville, if you were good enough you would go to the OHA. The season I played for Thetford Mines, we won the championship, and five of us from that team, including Reggie Houle, Marc Tardif and myself, went to the Montreal Junior Canadiens. We had such a great team in Montreal, we went on to win two Memorial Cups there."

The dominance of the Junior Canadiens, who defeated St. Catharines in the OHA finals, kept the Black Hawks from winning any hardware; however, the team had far exceeded its recent performances, while Dionne surpassed all expectations. He credits the pressure-free environment created by the people who surrounded him. Aware of how sensitive he was through those years, Marcel urges coaches of today to recognize that all players need to be given the opportunity to understand not only the physical demands of the game, but the mental dimension as well.

"I was one of those guys that took everything personally. Although you think you can handle criticism, what you need is someone to explain what is going on. Over my career I had teammates who would look at a younger player and comment on the immaturity of that person, and I'm thinking, 'Well, who is taking him aside and explaining what's what?'

"For example, if a player comes along who is really cocky, many veterans didn't like that in a rookie. Myself, I believe cockiness, if used in the right manner, can be a good thing. I would say to the veteran, 'This guy thinks he's good. Well, let's let him be good. That's what we're looking for, right? He's going to calm down.' But a lot of guys would say, 'Ahhh.' And I would tell them, 'You watch—if he is a genuine person, with kindness in him, that's what we want. Maybe he has no other way to express himself.' To me, I laugh about it. I like someone who is a little cocky—so long as they can back it up. If it turns out that he's cocky and he can't deliver, then he comes down twice as hard. But I've always given people that chance. Show me, so I understand. And I'll say, 'He's all right. That's just his way.'

"The challenge that coaches face is to be able to teach kids. The problem facing kids is that many coaches are not good teachers. It's a difficult task to keep a pack of players together and make them a successful team. In attempting to do this, coaches seldom look at the individual. We all have different ideas and personalities that come into play. I know that I would have benefited from somebody taking me aside and explaining constructive criticism, and criticism in coaching. Not everybody responds to being yelled at. Not everybody can handle being screamed at in front of his or her peers. Some people simply can't take it; others are able to respond to it.

"Unfortunately, I think a lot of coaches aren't qualified to deal with this properly. As a result they hurt, and in some cases lose, a lot of young people. It's important to have a good start for whatever you aspire to in life. When I played minor hockey, and even in junior, I wasn't certain that I'd make it in the NHL. I don't care what anybody says, I didn't know! To get there, to reach your goals, self-esteem is very important."

With the accomplishments of his first season in St. Catharines under his belt, a girlfriend he was very much in love with, and a group of teammates who were also close friends, Marcel's life couldn't have been better. Upon returning to Drummondville to work for the summer, he was also grateful to be reunited with his family. But over the course of that summer Marcel came to realize that as much as he loved being home, St. Catharines held all that he longed for. The greatest of these desires was Carol. "He left me that summer and wrote to me. And I kept all of his love letters. He said to me, 'Don't ever show these to anybody, they'll think I'm crazy. I love you so much. You are the girl I'm going to marry.'" Carol smiles. "I told him, 'You *are* crazy.'"

The early years of their relationship were a delightful and inno-cent time. Busy with hockey and school, Marcel still had plenty of time for Carol. In their circle of friends they were the ideal couple, Carol the ever-polite lady and Marcel the perfect gentleman. Fre-quenting many social gatherings with the team, Marcel became notorious for his abstention from alcohol. There was virtually no recreational drinking in his first season, while in his last two years he became open to moderation. "When it came to drinking, I had no interest at that time. Some people drink, some people never drink. It's funny, with all the beer I was exposed to over the years, that I never had a beer before I was seventeen or eighteen. And I came from a drinking family—I mean heavy drinkers. But I just wasn't interested."

"Marcel's first beer at my house was over Christmastime," Carol recalls. "One night when he was staying late my stepfather offered him a beer. It must have taken him six hours to drink it."

Feeling more at ease with his English, by Marcel's second season he was spending a great deal of time with his teammates. In partic-ular, two players, goaltender George Hulme and forward Brian McKenzie, became quite close to him. The highlight of the week for the gang came after their regular home game. "Sunday night was the big night. George, myself, Brian and a couple of other friends, we would bring the girls and meet at a friend's house after our game. We'd order pizza and have a couple of beers; that was the big thing. All the guys were going to school at the time and we played or practised during the week, so that was the best time for everyone to get together. Boy, those were fun days."

While the Sunday postgame gatherings were laid-back affairs, that wasn't always the case year round. As an annual tradition on the Victoria Day weekend in May, Brian McKenzie hosted a spring bash at his parents' summer retreat in Bancroft, Ontario. Alcohol consumption was never a prerequisite for Marcel to have a good time, and he was clearly comfortable with this policy. However, when his mirthful buddies were fit to party, Marcel's relative tameness presented an irresistible opportunity for pranksterism.

"Every year we'd get twelve guys to go up," McKenzie remembers. "We called it the Dirty Dozen. For the entire weekend all we did was drink beer, play ball hockey in the pasture and throw each other in the river. So one year Marce came up. He arrives on the first night of this weekend, and of course everybody's pumped up and pounding back the beer. Marce has a couple of beers and at about ten o'clock he decides he wants to go to bed.

"Well, once he gets up in the bunk the guys start spraying shaving cream on his face and sticking cigarettes in his ears. Basically, we were totally harassing him. Marcel gets up, looks down from the bunk at everyone, and says, 'I will get even with you.' And he repeats it: 'I *will* get even with you.' Finally, the guys let him go to sleep. Well, at five o'clock in the morning Marce is up and wide awake. He's got two pots and he's standing in the middle of the cottage banging these pots together, yelling, 'À LA SOUPE! À LA SOUPE, YOU BASTARDS!' Like, 'Come and get it,' right? You never screwed with Marcel, because he'd always get you."

Chapter Three

A S WAS THE CASE in Dionne's first year, the Montreal Junior Canadiens were once again the team to beat in 1969–70. Despite another banner year, in which Dionne led the league in points for the first time, St. Catharines was no match for Montreal's depth. The Junior Canadiens eliminated the Black Hawks in the OHA semifinals before defeating the Toronto Marlboros and Weyburn Red Wings to claim their second Memorial Cup championship—becoming only the third team in history to win back-to-back titles. The good news for Dionne and his Black Hawks, however, was that Montreal's core talent had finally outgrown the junior ranks. The following season would be an entirely different story.

By the fall of 1970, Gilbert Perreault, Marc Tardif and Réjean Houle had all begun their NHL careers, leaving a gaping hole in the Junior Canadiens' front line. With Montreal no longer posing as formidable a threat, St. Catharines' stiffest competition would come from the Toronto Marlboros. And the Marlboros had a team that was up for the challenge. Led by a triple threat of their own in Dave Gardner, Billy Harris and Steve Shutt, they were the new pacesetters.

"I don't think I've ever been a great individual player," Steve Shutt admits. "My strength was that I've always been able to fit in playing with somebody else. When I went to the Montreal Canadiens, obviously playing with the guy on the right side [Guy Lafleur]—well, everybody knew what he could do. And I'd just finish off from him. In junior it was the same thing but with Dave Gardner and Billy Harris. Harris was a big right winger, you know; he was the strength on the line. Then there was Dave Gardner, who was the finesse guy, and I was the finisher."

In the final year of his junior career, every player aspiring to make the NHL is focused on performing to the best of his abilities. For Marcel Dionne, there was no better way to prove his worth than to lead his team to the Memorial Cup—the junior hockey championship of all of Canada. To beat the likes of the Marlboros he would have to have the season of his life. As the team's chief offensive threat, that would mean adding the twin feathers of a scoring title and a national championship to his cap. However, while he set about that task in St. Catharines, his counterpart Dave Gardner had similar designs in Toronto.

Being the dominant player on the Black Hawks made Marcel a clear target, but his diminutive size and incredible speed consistently outmatched those opponents assigned to stop him. And when he was forced to stand his ground with an aggressor, it was those very same assets, backed by the proverbial fight in the dog, which proved Dionne the better. Brian McKenzie witnessed just how handy Marcel was on those rare occasions that he was tested. "He didn't drop the gloves many times, but I'll tell you, when he did, he could sure handle himself. I'll tell you one guy that Marcel beat the crap out of was a fellow by the name of Owen Jelly. He played for Niagara Falls and then for the Hamilton Red Wings. Obviously, he did something to Marcel first, because Marcel would never start a fight. Well, Marcel threw 'em quick, and with both hands! He just pummelled the shit out of this guy. I'll never forget that, the night Marce beat up O.J."

When asked about the fights he had in junior, Marcel countered, with a smile, "I remember every goal." After some prodding, Dionne spoke of the fight McKenzie described, as well as a more recent—and much friendlier—meeting with Owen Jelly. "I've seen that guy since—I ran into to him at a dinner. I looked at him, and he came up to me, and we had a laugh about that fight. Then I went over to sit with his family. He still remembers it—and I felt bad about it. But he told me that it was his claim to fame. And I said, 'Well, if you feel that way, that some good came of it, then that's a good way of looking at it.' When we went to the penalty box he almost suckered me. I didn't see it coming, so we got up, the sweaters came off and we went at it again. The next time I saw him, he had a nice shiner. But I was always pretty good about walking away from that type of thing. You take a cheap shot and fight through it. In a way, I was fortunate. I didn't break my nose from fighting, I broke it from high sticks or a puck hitting it."

With all of the Black Hawks' horses bursting out of the gates, the 1970–71 season looked like one in which they could go all the way. As the season progressed, each victory became more important than the one before. And whenever the Marlboros provided the opposition, the Hawks' motivation and desire increased tenfold. Undoubtedly, the same was true in the Toronto dressing room. A member of the Marlies that season, Glenn Goldup, recalls the focus of the team's game plan whenever they faced St. Catharines. "Every time you thought of going to St. Catharines there was only one guy you had in mind, and that was Marcel Dionne. All of the team meetings we had prior to playing the Junior Black Hawks centred around Marcel and how we'd stop him. Because he would get a couple of goals and a couple of assists *every* night. It was unbelievable. For his size and proximity to the ice it was just amazing. He was magic."

In his role as an aggressive player on the Marlboros, every time Goldup got the chance to finish a check against Dionne he did so with enthusiasm. It was this thoroughness that resulted in a spirit-crushing injury to Marcel, which placed his shot at the scoring title in grave danger.

"I remember one game in particular, which was the night that I broke Marcel's collarbone," says Goldup. "It was midseason. Basically, I went into the corner with him and hit him pretty good; that was my game. I actually lifted him off the ice, into the boards, and down he went. And you could tell that was it. I mean, his wing was hanging. I knew I got him good because I could feel his feet leave the ice. Well, as soon as you feel a guy's feet leave the ice, you've got complete control. So when I put him into the boards I proceeded to make sure I got a good lick on him. As it turned out, I did get a pretty good lick on him and broke his collarbone.

"But the hit wasn't vindictive toward Marcel. It was, 'Way to go. That was a good hit.' It also relieved us from having to face Marcel because we had a couple of other games against them during his recovery. Obviously, that was a big bonus for us because we were running hard for the Memorial Cup. We had good teams in those days, so we were always trying to get there. But it wasn't easy when Marcel was on the ice. After that incident, Tommy Smythe [the general manager of the Toronto Marlboros and son of Leafs owner Stafford Smythe] took me out to dinner. I think I had a couple of good weeks and was playing very well and he was just rewarding me for that effort. The fact that I put Marcel Dionne out of commission was more or less the icing on the cake."

For Marcel, the injury represented another setback in a list of obstacles that seemed to be preventing him from getting the complete recognition he deserved. After experiencing the frustration of an abbreviated first season due to the league transfer, his second season should have alleviated any dissatisfaction. Although he had beaten out Gilbert Perreault for the 1969–70 scoring title, he had lost the league MVP honours that same year to Perreault. It being Perreault's final season of junior hockey, the award was arguably given to him in recognition of a spectacular junior career. Now, in *his* final year of junior, Marcel's broken collarbone threatened to deny him the same consideration.

"I went up to the boards and Goldie hit me and my collarbone snapped. Well, I was devastated," Dionne sighs. "I thought, 'Holy shit, this is ridiculous.' It was another thing that, emotionally, I couldn't handle. It was tough because I knew we had a good team and I thought that this was our year. I cried for a day. Eventually, I decided that staying in St. Catharines wasn't doing me any good, so I went home to Drummondville. It was my first time with a major injury and I didn't know how to deal with it. When you break your collarbone, basically it just has to heal by itself. Instead of staying in St. Catharines and moping around the team, I opted for a change of scene and a fresh look at things. So I went home.

"I just didn't want to be around the guys. I was totally depressed and shocked by it all. I acted like a kid—I *was* a kid. When you're hurt, it's almost like you're in the way. We all know that. Just like we know that when you're injured, somebody else takes your job. Sooner or later, everybody gets hurt and everybody goes through that feeling. That's all part of it, and I believe that's okay. But I don't think you need to be in the dressing room to cheer the guys on. That's absolutely false.

"I needed to stay away from the team to get my mind together. I remember the general manager called me, and I was crying on the phone. I told him that I thought my career was over. I couldn't get a hold of myself. He said, 'Marcel, we'd like you to come back to be with the team, to be in the dressing room.' I said, 'I can't.' I could barely speak. I was devastated. That was a time of crisis in my life that I had no experience in dealing with. What I needed was somebody to take me aside and say, 'Listen, it happens to everybody. This is what your recovery time is, and when you get back, your collarbone is going to be as strong as before.'"

In his absence, Dionne's teammates picked up their game. In particular, Marcel's close friend Brian McKenzie took it upon himself to lead the team. Not only did McKenzie succeed in that regard, he actually propelled himself into the scoring race. With each game, Marcel fell further behind. And with a projected recovery time of four to six weeks, his chances of making up the lost ground seemed remote at best. Glued to the sports page, he would read the stories and do the math. Needless to say, he was not pleased to be watching from afar. Winning the scoring title was not simply a point of pride for Marcel; it was a confirmation that he was ready for the next phase of his career: the National Hockey League.

Once his collarbone started to feel better, Marcel put on his skates and took to the outdoor rink in the old schoolyard. Soon after, he returned to St. Catharines with every intention of getting his team to the Memorial Cup. And if he could somehow win the scoring title in the process, perhaps he would receive the credit he had missed out on the year before. The fact that his team had done remarkably well without him had his competitive blood on full boil; his desire to return could not have been stronger.

"When Marcel was hurt, we only lost a couple of games in his absence," Brian McKenzie points out with a measure of satisfaction. "Our goalie, George Hulme, knows the facts better than I do. I say that because every summer when we get together for our reunion golf tournament, Hulmey will get half-pissed on the Friday night and start with the digs directed at Marce. 'Hey, Brian, how many games did we lose with Marcel out of the lineup? Remember?' Marcel will be standing there and I'm telling George to shut up. But Marcel, George and I were like brothers. We played together for three years and hung around together in the summer. I mean, I used to lend Marcel my '57 Pontiac to pick up Carol from the French school in Welland; you know, they went out together from day one. But we had our fights and arguments, too.

"I remember when he got injured; he was our captain and he wouldn't even come in our dressing room. But we knew what he was going through. He's a very proud person and he was the leader of our team. And I don't believe he would have been happier if we lost all of the games he missed, but I think he felt we revelled a little too much in the fact that we did so well without him.

"At that time, Dave Gardner, myself and Rick Martin were jockeying back and forth for the scoring lead when Marcel was hurt. So when Marce was out they wrote a story—and again, I attributed his reaction to Marcel not having a full understanding of the English language. I had said in the article that because Marcel was hurt, the rest of the team had to take up the slack. And everybody did. I think he took it as me saying that *we don't need* Marcel Dionne because everybody else took up the slack. So Marcel came to me when he returned—and I don't think he would deny this—he said, 'I will beat you for the scoring championship.' And I said, 'I hope you do! We want to win.'"

As teammates and friends, Brian and Marcel shared the same goal. As competitors, Marcel was accustomed to being the dark horse, and he behaved as such. In hindsight, he acknowledges the boldness of his manner, which went unchecked due to his independent circumstances. "Because I was on my own, nobody really guided me. I did things on my own every day, so whatever I did or said, I figured that it was okay because nobody ever reprimanded me. I love a challenge, but I will say that I probably stepped out of bounds when I said that to Brian about the scoring race. He took over the team and played so well. He made such a big difference; I was shocked. Before then, he was the comic on the team—and suddenly you see his leadership. He really took his role seriously, which kind of sent me a wake-up call. But we respected each other very much, and that's why we stayed friends."

Upon Marcel's return to St. Catharines, Carol was also determined to see him bounce back. Knowing that her boyfriend was in need of a boost, she enthused that he was not out of the scoring race just yet. "That was a tough season for Marcel. The guy that was leading the league in scoring was Dave Gardner. He was ahead of Marcel by about twenty points. But I always stood behind Marcel. My mother and I would sit down and calculate how many points Marcel needed per game to pass him."

Once he returned to the lineup, Dionne took off immediately; he put up numbers at an inconceivable rate and, despite the odds, earned the scoring title for the second straight year. Capping off his final year of junior, Marcel Dionne scored an amazing 62 goals and 81 assists for 143 points in just 46 games. Since 1945–46, when the OHA began awarding the Eddie Powers Memorial Trophy to its top scorer, no player had ever won it in back-to-back seasons. Glenn Goldup and the rest of the Toronto Marlboros were astonished by what had transpired. "Marcel was out for five or six weeks, during which Dave Gardner had caught up and passed him. Well, doesn't Marcel come back and beat him anyway."

Brian McKenzie: "Now we laugh about it, and I'll say, 'Yeah, Frank put you out there for the power play, penalty killing—you played the whole game. No wonder you beat me!' But seriously, he was just fantastic. He came back from that injury and said, 'I *will* beat you for the scoring championship,' and he did. [McKenzie ended up with 124 points in 60 games, good for second place on the Hawks and fourth in the OHA.] I've often wondered what he would have finished with if he'd have played the entire season."

Over his three years with the St. Catharines Black Hawks, Marcel had not only proved himself as the league's best goal scorer, he had also established his presence in the dressing room. Endorsing him as the total package, Brian McKenzie related his teammate's attention to detail in preparing his team for each game. "Marcel knew the game. He wasn't just a good player. He was aware of the strengths and weaknesses on each of the teams we were up against. I'll never forget in our final year when we played the Kitchener Rangers in the playoffs; Marcel told us, believe it or not, to go down Larry Robinson's side. When he played junior, Larry Robinson couldn't turn to the outside. He was a little weak on the skating. And Marcel always knew the deficiencies of the other teams and what we should look for. In our last year, Marcel had a lot of confidence."

As the playoffs unfolded, the Black Hawks were inevitably matched with the Toronto Marlboros for the league championship. Setting the stage for the confrontation of the league's two dominant teams was the announcement of the Red Tilson Trophy winner, the OHA's most valuable player. To the surprise of every junior hockey fan, the award went to the Marlboros' Dave Gardner.

Prior to the opening game of the series at Maple Leaf Gardens, in a ceremony evidently designed to give the home team an emotional lift, Gardner was presented with his trophy. As Marcel recalls, it was an awkward moment. "It was the first game of the series in Toronto, and right at centre ice they gave the MVP award to Dave Gardner. That was the Red Tilson Trophy awarded by the Toronto sportswriters. The people in Maple Leaf Gardens were booing the decision. And they asked me to centre ice to shake hands with him. I remember telling Dave not to worry about it; that's the way life goes."

The events that followed would make the voters who misappropriated the honour from Dionne look as foolish as their decision. In short order, Marcel and his mates made their case. "Well, they had a very good team, but we kicked their asses four straight. We were the underdogs, and the Marlies had a really good team, but we just smoked 'em. Every time I see Steve Shutt I remind him, 'You won your four Stanley Cups, but we killed you guys in junior.' I remember the last goal I scored." He sneers. "It was the last goal of the game, there was an open net, and I had about ten feet and I smoked it in the top corner with a slapshot, just to say thank you very much."

As he tells the story of that playoff series, Dionne exudes the pride of a competitor who strove to win every time he laced up the skates. Does the absence of the Red Tilson Trophy from Dionne's résumé bother him? Absolutely. And so it should. If such slights or setbacks didn't bother players of his ilk, there would be no need for a Hall of Fame. Nevertheless, being cheated out of a pat on the back didn't stall the Dionne engine. He recovered to lead his team in a decisive victory over the favourites. However, the question does linger: Why, when it was blatantly clear to everyone else that he deserved it, was Marcel Dionne denied the league's MVP award?

"He was too short," Steve Shutt cracks. "That's all it was. People don't like short guys."

Shutt can afford to be facetious; it's a privilege of his friendship with Marcel. But he continues in a more serious vein, offering what he saw as a reality of the game in Toronto. "Obviously, it's a bigger media centre, and at the time the Leafs weren't doing very well. As a result there was a lot of focus put on our line. Geez, I think we were averaging 8,000 people per game in attendance; for a couple of games we had 12,000 people there. It was great, we loved it!"

Glenn Goldup, who went on to play with Marcel in Los Angeles and remains a good friend, concurred with Shutt, giving the

Marlies' top forward line additional credit. "The only reason that I can think of for Marcel not getting the MVP, as I look back on it, was because of the year that Steve Shutt had—scoring 70 goals. On that line of Billy Harris, Dave Gardner and Steve Shutt, Gardner was definitely the quarterback. I mean, the level of their game just went through the roof when they grabbed Gardner and put him between Shutt and Harris. And you've got to attribute the 70-goal season Shutt had to the play of Dave Gardner; it was a perfect combination. Gards would feed Shutty at the perfect time, and Shutty had that awesome shot. The other factor against Marcel would be the St. Catharines-versus-Toronto thing. You always seemed to get a little edge in Toronto. But there is no way that Marce didn't deserve the MVP. When you consider the season he had, I think it's an amazing tale."

After the exhilaration of beating the Toronto Marlboros, the St. Catharines Black Hawks entered what would become one of the most infamous series in the history of junior hockey. As the league champions of the OHA, St. Catharines were slated to play their counterparts in the Quebec Major Junior Hockey League, the Quebec Remparts. The matchup between these two teams had earned an incredible amount of ink due to the participation of the top two prospects in the coming NHL draft, Guy Lafleur and Marcel Dionne. For years this French-Canadian duo had been forecast to become the superstars of the next era in the NHL. The question that fascinated the commentators of the day was which of them would be the first to go in the draft.

Having played his entire junior career in Quebec, Lafleur was the favourite amongst the majority of French-Canadians. In the opposite corner, Marcel, who had left Quebec to play in Ontario, was depicted as a traitor in his home province. Although he had felt the sting of this sentiment since his departure, it was about to be amplified and exploited in a manner he had never dreamed possible.

At that time there existed in the province of Quebec a volatile political climate that was heating up. In the spring of 1971, memories were still fresh of the October 1970 FLQ crisis, during which the provincial labour and immigration minister, Pierre Laporte, had been kidnapped and murdered. Tensions ran high, and relations between French and English political bodies were strained, to say the least. Unfortunately, against this backdrop, the high drama of junior hockey was fashioned into a pressure valve for certain hostile parties to let off steam.

In St. Catharines for the opening game, the sense of rivalry between Ontario and Quebec electrified the capacity crowd. Bill Bird, who broadcast the series, witnessed a prank which, aimed as a slight against the French-Canadian players and fans, got the series off on the wrong foot. "Some lout got some frogs and threw them on the ice. I mean, come on, Marcel was from Quebec, too. And let's face it, the Quebec league had a history of not being able to win the Memorial Cup, and here they had this superstar in Guy Lafleur, who they worshipped. So for somebody to pull a stunt like that, it probably didn't help matters."

From that point on, the series devolved into a sideshow that had little to do with the showdown taking place on the ice. Nevertheless, the Remparts and Black Hawks tried to remain focused on the games. Having never played one another, the two sides were mutually unfamiliar, although every player was sensibly alerted to the other team's greatest threat.

"My vivid memory of our series against Quebec was that we didn't know what to expect," says goalie George Hulme. "We'd never seen their hockey team, never seen Lafleur. And it wasn't just Lafleur we had to worry about. They also had Jacques Richard and André Savard; they had a good hockey team. But all we ever heard about was Guy Lafleur.

"The first two games were in St. Catharines. The opening game, they beat us in the third period [Remparts 4, Black Hawks 2]. They had a goaltender, Michel Deguise, who really was outstanding in the series. But in the next game we crushed them, 8–3.

Marcel was incredible, and to me, it really looked like he was over-shadowing Lafleur in the series head to head. I mean, this was it—the big confrontation! Then we went to Quebec City."

After splitting the first two games in St. Catharines, the venue shifted to the Remparts' home ice at the Colisée in Quebec City. Deguise, the goaltender who had been so beatable in game two, regained his stellar form of the first game. The rules for the series stipulated that each team could conscript the best goalie from their respective league, regardless of which team he had played for throughout the season. The Black Hawks, for better or for worse, declined the option. The Remparts, however, picked up Deguise from Sorel, and succeeded in gaining an edge between the pipes.

"We could have picked up Bunny Larocque from the Ottawa 67s, but George Hulme had played for us for three years without a backup," Brian McKenzie defends. "I didn't think it was fair to bring in somebody else, and our entire team agreed. So we went with George. It wasn't that George didn't stop the puck for us; it was this damn Michel Deguise. In the first game we outshot them something like 62–31. Those numbers may not be right, but it was double to what they had. And they still beat us. He was unbeliev-able. I'll tell you, in his life, that was his fifteen minutes of fame—and he ruined ours."

Hot goaltending proved to be only a part of the challenge for the Black Hawks. Upon arriving in Quebec City, the St. Catharines contingent discovered another obstacle to contend with. The utter disdain of certain French-Canadians for their English visi-tors was felt by the team and their fans at all points of contact, especially in the Colisée. While watching the series with the fami-lies of Marcel's teammates, Laurette Dionne fielded the barbs in stride. "When the people in the stands heard the St. Catharines booster club conversing in English, they said, 'You don't speak English here, you speak French!' Then they said, 'We're also going to teach that Dionne how to speak French!' There was a lot of anger with a lot of people then due to the FLQ [the Front de libération du Québec]."

But what was a day-to-day reality for the Dionne family was a slap in the face for many players on the St. Catharines Black Hawks. Few of them had experienced the crude ferocity of a French-Canadian ripping.

"The first sign of ill will on the trip to Quebec was with the bus driver," Brian McKenzie recalls. "They picked us up at the airport and there was some difficulty in communicating with the driver, who wouldn't speak English. Marcel called him on it, on him refusing to speak English, and they got into an argument. But that was nothing compared to the reception we got at the arena.

"I would say there were approximately 3,500 people scattered about the Colisée when we arrived. There were no lights on, and we were just waiting by the gate, checking out the arena before our game—we'd never been there before. So we're looking at the ice and these people are up in the stands yelling, 'Hey, Dionne, f— off!' 'Hey, Guité, you c—sucker!' I'm telling you, these guys were sitting there with their families. So Marcel says to us, 'Well, that's not swearing to them. In the French language, you swear against the church. Their swear words aren't your swear words.' We're all standing there laughing like, What the hell is this? Look at this guy. He's got his kids with him, and he's telling Marcel to f— off, he's calling Pierre [Guité] a c—sucker, and it's coming from all over the building. Anyway, when the game started it was obvious that there was no way we were getting out of there with a win."

As the first game in the Colisée progressed, the level of sportsmanship on the ice declined. And at the conclusion of the Remparts' 3–1 victory, the series officially turned ugly at the hands of Brian McKenzie. Dissatisfied with the number of penalties called against his team, he resolved to express his displeasure with the officiating. As the linesmen and referee were leaving the ice surface, he charged at the officials and cross-checked them through the gate. For his actions, McKenzie earned a suspension and sat out the next game.

Tempers ran high, and the participation—or interference—of the fans clearly made matters worse. Although Marcel Dionne expected a rough ride, he was disappointed that the series had become a circus of abuse and violence. "There were too many distractions for us to play. Things were constantly being thrown on the ice. We had a couple of tough guys in Pierre Guité and Mike Bloom. Well, as soon as there was a fight the fans would start launching missiles. They were throwing D-cell batteries; we were lucky nobody got hurt. The thing that really aggravated the team was the abuse the booster club and our parents took—verbal and physical! There were even death-threat telephone calls made to my house. That was a very emotional time; it was French versus English. There was also the anticipation of who would be number one, Flower or me. I still have a picture of the two of us at Maple Leaf Gardens. People wanted to get our picture together, the two best players in junior."

Predictably, the abuse that took place in the stands in game three escalated in game four. Sentenced to watch the game from the stands for his own gross misconduct, Brian McKenzie took the brunt of the Remparts fans' wrath. "Whatever they could get their hands on, they threw at our bench. I remember one of the items that landed on us was a woman's wig that was sewn shut, stuffed with two apples and a mickey bottle inside it. They threw nail clippers with the pointed end open . . . ball bearings. . . . The second game in Quebec, I sat in the worst possible place, behind our bench. I had ice cream bars just dripping off me."

This time the Remparts defeated the Black Hawks handily, 6–1, taking a 3–1 lead over St. Catharines in the series. Under normal circumstances, most hockey teams hope to emerge from a two-game set on the road with a win. But the St. Catharines Black Hawks found themselves literally hoping to escape with their lives.

"They beat us the second game in the Colisée; we were leaving the ice and it was crazy," says McKenzie. "So Marcel says, 'Don't go up in the stands. Bring your father, bring your brother, and we'll all go across the ice together.' So we get across the ice and, as we're going under the exit to the dressing room, somebody fires some garbage at Mike Bloom's head. In retaliation, Bloomer

Marcel (far right) at age eight with his younger siblings, Rénald and Linda.

Marcel as a Drummondville peewee.

Posing with the hardware.

The team captain hoists the trophy.

Marcel fills the cup at a victory rehearsal. Brian McKenzie is on
Marcel's right, and George Hulme is wearing the hat.

The real thing: St. Catharines Black Hawks defeat the
Toronto Marlboros, winning the OHA championship in 1971.

Marcel with buddies Brian McKenzie and George Hulme.

Dionne began his career in Detroit without a helmet.

Team Canada 1972, a great experience and honour for the young Dionne.

Eager to succeed in Detroit.

With player agent Alan Eagleson.

Carol and Marcel on their wedding day, April 5, 1974.

comes up with his stick, chopping up from underneath the exit. Well, guess what? He cranks a cop—right over the eye! Then all hell broke loose. So we got everyone into the dressing room and Marcel says, 'Lock the doors. Don't let them take Bloomer because they'll beat the shit out of him.'

"Finally we got changed and were ready to leave; the police got all of the information on Bloomer and they agreed not to take him to jail. So, the head of the detectives comes in and says, 'Okay, we're getting ready. We've got the police out there and we're going to get you on your bus and get you out of here.' They told us to get our bags and we're all going to leave together. Well, just before we go out the door he comes back and tells us we have to wait because they blew a tire on our bus. And we're thinking, 'How do you blow a tire on a bus? You can't get through it with a knife. Do they have guns?' Then he returns and informs us that it's one of the tires on the back, and there are two tires back there, so we're going anyway.

"They had our bus pulled up right against the building, so when we walked out of the door it was right onto the bus. Once we're on the bus, then it really starts—rocks, bottles, windows are breaking. There's a mob of 2,500 in the parking lot firing stuff at us. And we had this old fellow, Harry Argent; he was one of our trainers. He had to be seventy years old. Harry gets on the bus and the poor guy is lying on the floor trying to stay out of harm's way when Bloomer gets on. Harry sees Bloomer and yells out, 'You get away from me. You're the one they want!' Bloomer just goes, 'Ahh, f— off, Harry,' and steps over him and goes to the back of the bus. Meanwhile, the windows are smashing and we're all lying down. It was a surreal experience.

"Eventually we pulled into our motel and spent the night sitting between the two beds because we thought the FLQ was going to send a bomb through the window. We were happy to get out of there alive."

Back in Ontario, the demand for tickets forced St. Catharines' next home game to be moved to Toronto's Maple Leaf Gardens.

In front of a sellout crowd, the Black Hawks bounced back, defeating the Remparts 6–3. The victory put them right back in the series and, ideally, on a plane to Quebec. However, the hostile conditions they had faced there posed a serious dilemma for the parents, who were concerned for the safety of their boys.

Because much of the animosity had been directed at the two French-Canadian Black Hawks, the question was put to Pierre Guité and Marcel Dionne: Did they want to continue the series if it meant returning to Quebec City?

"The team had requested that the remaining games be played at a neutral site and suggested the Montreal Forum," Dionne explains. "Even though it was still in [the province of] Quebec, the Remparts refused. It came down to a vote and Pierre Guité and myself were willing to go back to Quebec City. It was reported that the players didn't want to finish the series; the reality was that the *parents* didn't want the team to go back. It was a scary situation."

Regrettably, the series that showcased the two brightest prospects for the upcoming NHL draft was never settled. Marcel and his teammates begrudge the fact to this day, but there was little they could do. What made the outcome even more bitter was the opportunity they handed over to the Remparts.

"The series we played the Remparts in that year was supposed to be for the eastern provincial championship," George Hulme says. "This is what the OHA told us all along. Because out west they were using over-age juniors—twenty-one-year-olds—there was not going to be a Memorial Cup that year. So, really, we were playing for the eastern Canadian Junior A title against Quebec. As it happened, we forfeited the series, and then Quebec invited the Edmonton Oil Kings, who had won the west, to come to Quebec City with all expenses paid. They told them, 'Let's play a two-out-of-three for the Memorial Cup,' which wasn't supposed to be awarded at all that year. Quebec won two straight, and that's how the Remparts won the Memorial Cup."

In the eyes of the St. Catharines players, the invitation and the cordial treatment Quebec extended to the Oil Kings were the hockey equivalent of inviting lambs to the slaughter. "I remember when I played for the Edmonton Oilers [in the World Hockey Association], and Bill Hunter was the coach; he owned the Oil Kings when they played Quebec for the Memorial Cup," Brian McKenzie recalls. "We were on an airplane once, and he made a comment about how the guys from the OHA wouldn't go into Quebec and finish that series. And I mean, I've gotten in trouble the odd time for my tongue. I looked right back at him and said, 'Bill, the only reason Quebec treated you guys so well was because they knew they'd beat you in two games. *We* were a threat to them. You guys—you were *no* threat!' He didn't respond very well to that."

Chapter Four

NOT LONG AFTER the playoff series between St. Catharines and Quebec met its premature end, the fates of both teams' captains—Marcel Dionne and Guy Lafleur—were to be decided in the National Hockey League's 1971 amateur draft. Out of respect and admiration, Dionne's family and friends hoped that he would be the first player to be selected. Certainly, everyone who had seen him dominate the Ontario Hockey Association, winning back-to-back scoring titles and leading the Black Hawks to the league championship, would have been inclined to agree.

The draft was intended to give the NHL's weakest clubs the first crack at the most talented players in junior and college hockey. A powerful team like the Montreal Canadiens—who in the spring of '71 won their fifth Stanley Cup title in seven years—were supposed to wait their turn. But Sam Pollock, Montreal's general manager, was determined that his team would draft one of the two budding francophone superstars. In May 1970, he began laying the groundwork by making a trade with the woeful California (formerly Oakland) Seals, who surrendered their first-round pick in 1971. So poor was the Seals' on-ice performance that it was virtually guaranteed this would give the Habs the first choice overall.

By the middle of the 1970–71 season, however, it looked as if Pollock's plan might be going awry; the Los Angeles Kings, and not the Seals, were threatening to inhabit the NHL basement. It was time for the Canadiens to cover their bets; on January 26, 1971, they dealt the veteran centreman Ralph Backstrom to L.A. in exchange for a couple of spare parts, Gord Labossière and Ray Fortin. Peter Mahovlich, who was in his first full season with the Canadiens, recalls what happened next.

"What it did was, it helped Los Angeles get ahead of Oakland, so Oakland ended up getting first pick in the draft, which happened to go to Montreal. Sam had a game plan, and he implemented that by helping other teams. They picked Guy Lafleur in the draft, but it wouldn't have been a mistake picking Marcel Dionne."

After a frustrating conclusion to what had been a magnificent junior career, Dionne was concerned about the possibility of being drafted by the Canadiens. Still a young man brimming with emotion, he was unsettled by the thought of heading into the pressure cooker that Montreal was known to be. Add the strain of being the next superstar in a glorious history of Montreal legends and the situation amounted to one that Marcel saw as a poor fit.

When draft day arrived, the Dionne family received a phone call from a friend in the Canadiens organization that put their minds at ease. "I was a good friend of [the Forum public address announcer] Claude Mouton, who was a legend in Montreal," Marcel recalls. "He followed me from when I played peewee and bantam and always liked me, but he called my mom at 7:30 in the morning and told her that Lafleur was going to go first. He told her that he liked me and they tried everything, and he just wanted to let us know. So that was good of him to do. But it didn't matter to me. I didn't even want to go to Montreal. And Montreal tried to get me by trying to get the first and second pick. But looking back, Detroit [who drafted him second overall] was the right place for me to go. If I had gone to Montreal I probably would have committed suicide—jumped off the Jacques Cartier Bridge. I had too much emotion; they would have destroyed me in Montreal."

Nor was there any doubt in the province of Quebec that the Canadiens had drafted wisely. The great Montreal sportscaster, Dick Irvin, felt just how strong the attraction for Lafleur was in French Canada. "When they were drafted one and two, I think Dionne was lost in the shuffle in Montreal, I really do—for two reasons. Number one, Marcel didn't play his junior in Quebec—he wasn't playing in their backyard. He went to play in St.

Catharines, so he wasn't in their face as a junior player leading up to the draft. And you know they are very provincial here. The second reason was Lafleur. I mean, Lafleur was *the* guy in Quebec. It would have been interesting had Dionne and Lafleur played against each other in the Quebec league. Then I think there would have been quite a hassle—I'm talking about the media. You might have had a Dionne camp and a Lafleur camp when it came time for the Canadiens to make their pick.

"But there was no question here in Quebec. If Sam Pollock had drafted Marcel Dionne, they would have run him out of town. There was absolutely no question that it was going to be Guy Lafleur. I remember the day of the draft—I was there. I guess it was the day after Jean Béliveau retired. And of course that's the story about Lafleur: Béliveau retired one day and the Canadiens drafted Lafleur the next. I think it was just so much Lafleur, and that was the whole story. And I don't think there was a blinking of an eye or wringing of hands that Marcel Dionne went to the Detroit Red Wings.

"The story was that Sam Pollock traded Ralph Backstrom to Los Angeles to make sure that L.A. could beat Oakland, then Oakland would finish in last place. Well, who's to say? I mean, what if Ralph Backstrom breaks his leg in his second game with Los Angeles? . . . And right from the time he made that deal it was Lafleur [he was after]. That's why he made the deal. It wasn't to get Marcel Dionne; it wasn't to get himself in a position to make a choice—there was no choice. In Montreal, Sam Pollock had absolutely no choice at all.

"And Sam Pollock is in no way a humorous man, but he made everybody laugh for the one and only time in his life when Clarence Campbell called for the first pick. Sam said, '*Time,* please, Mr. Campbell,' as if he needed more time to figure it out, and everybody laughed. So, of course it was Lafleur. And Marcel Dionne was lost in the shuffle and nobody gave it a second thought."

While the press and fans of Montreal may have dropped the

issue, it certainly wasn't the last Marcel Dionne would hear of it. Over the years, well-meaning fans have offered unsolicited sympathy that Dionne feels is both misguided and uncalled for. "When I got drafted, the issue was Dionne and Lafleur—two French-Canadians. And Montreal had a pretty powerful team back then. So when Lafleur was picked first, people asked me, 'How does it feel to be number two?' How do you respond to that question? What do you mean, how does it feel? It's all right; I'm not complaining.

"All through my career it's like people feel sorry for me. They tell me that it was too bad, that Montreal should have drafted me. Well, I played eighteen years in the NHL. What do you want me to do about it? If I had scored 200 goals and won ten Stanley Cups, would that make me a happier person? Or you score 700 goals and have no Stanley Cups? At the end of the day it doesn't matter, because that's the business of the game. The reality is that we can't *all* play for the Montreal Canadiens."

Contrary to the assumption that being drafted by the Detroit Red Wings was cause for disappointment, Dionne embraced the opportunity—and the challenges—it presented him. Both existed in ample amounts. Just as the torch in Montreal was to be passed from Béliveau to Lafleur, Dionne's arrival in the Motor City coincided with Gordie Howe's retirement. The need to fill that marquee void, coupled with the lack of depth on the Wings' roster, meant that Dionne would immediately see his fair share of ice time. By contrast, the Canadiens were notoriously patient in bringing their rookies along, usually requiring them to serve an apprenticeship in the minor leagues.

Hopeful, but by no means certain, that he would be able to meet the team's expectations, Marcel entered training camp uncertain as to how he would measure up in the big leagues. The competition for a roster spot would be sparse; many trades of questionable merit and motive had reduced Detroit to a subpar team. The state of a hockey team is ultimately gauged by its performance throughout the season and, in particular, the playoffs.

Suffice it to say that the Red Wings had room for improvement. Not only had they missed the playoffs in 1970–71, but they'd actually finished behind the two expansion clubs in Buffalo and Vancouver in the regular-season standings. The disarray within the Detroit "organization" was evident to Marcel as soon as he reported to training camp.

"The first day I went to camp with Detroit was a nightmare. It was not enjoyable, not at all what I thought it would be. The training camp was in Port Huron. I got there, and there were 110 guys skating on four different squads. Within the Red Wings organization they had minor-league teams in Virginia, Fort Worth and Port Huron. So, the first day you really don't know what's going on. I come in and I'm the last guy to get his physical done. By the time I got on the ice with the big team, they told me, 'It's too late, why don't you go next door (they had double rinks) and practise with the B squad?' By the time I got over there, laced up and got on the ice, the frickin' practice was over. That was my first day at training camp.

"Second day, guess what? I've got to go to Detroit for a press conference to introduce me to everybody, like I'm the next Gordie Howe—right. Then I return to Port Huron after missing the first two days of practice and I'm supposed to be practising with the big club. Now, everybody that practises with the big club dresses in the dressing room that's upstairs. Well, they had me dressing by myself downstairs, having no contact with the players upstairs. You could say I was ill at ease with the situation."

Without the opportunity to get his feet wet and prove to himself that he belonged with the big team, Marcel was left to ponder his doubts. He wondered why, if he was indeed going to be a key to the team's immediate future, he hadn't been welcomed to the dressing room he would be joining. Marcel's buddy from St. Catharines, George Hulme, roomed with him at that training camp. Hulme attributed the indifference towards Marcel to a dark cloud that hung over the Detroit Red Wings, in the person of Ned Harkness. "At that time, Ned Harkness, who had been the

Red Wings coach, had taken over as the big boss, the general manager. Ned was a college guy, rah-rah-rah; he coached at Cornell. I really believe that he thought Junior A players were second rate to his college players. And that's what he thought of Marcel. Well, the Red Wings didn't have a good team at that time, and here was a guy that could save their franchise. Marcel should have been given the red carpet treatment."

Impatient and eager to find his comfort zone, Marcel began to wonder if the NHL was the one hurdle he couldn't clear. "I called my dad, it was around the fifth day of training camp. I said, 'Dad, I'm not going to make it. They're too big and they're too strong.' I was only 168 pounds. My dad told me not to worry, that it would come. It was just a matter of time."

In time, Marcel came to realize that the not-so-amicable atmosphere at training camp was simply a product of people literally fighting one another for their jobs. Up to that point, he had never witnessed uncertainty of that nature in a dressing room. Contributing further to the unsettled team dynamic was the adjustment, not only to the moves management had made over the past season, but to the absence—for the first time in twenty-five years—of "Mr. Hockey," Gordie Howe.

Each member of the Red Wings had to navigate his own course through this time of transition, and Marcel took the matter of becoming a Red Wing into his own hands. To learn the ropes and gain insight into his new life, he looked to the experienced players to show him the way.

"I remember the first night the team went out to a restaurant to have a few drinks. The veterans would stick together, and the rookies would stick together. I remember saying, 'I'm not hanging around with the rookies, I'm going out with these guys; I want to know what it's all about.' And I did."

Beyond the team outings, Dionne stayed close to the other French-speaking players on the team, getting along particularly well with Guy Charron, Serge Lajeunesse and Léon Rochefort.

When the Red Wings camp in Port Huron concluded and the

team relocated to the neighbourhood of the old Detroit Olympia, Dionne's eyes opened wide. "It wasn't exactly a nice area of town. I had heard about it, but now I was there. I said, 'Holy Christ, I've never seen shacks like this before.' That was my first impression of Detroit. You come in on the Lodge Freeway and see Tiger Stadium and it's, 'Wow! This is the real deal.' And the Olympia is just sitting in a parking lot. You're looking around and there's no stores, nothing; there's a couple of houses here and there, but not much else. What's this old building doing here? And then you think, 'Well, Gordie Howe played there for all those years. It must be okay.'"

Having seen the lay of the land, Marcel's first priority became finding a place to live before his two weeks' hotel allowance ran out. Initially, he settled in with a family that Serge Lajeunesse was living with, not unlike the experience he had had as a boarder in his junior days. Shortly thereafter, teammate Nick Libett announced that he was moving from the house he had rented, and suggested to Marcel that he might consider taking it over. The move provided him with accommodations for houseguests should any of his family come to visit. Living on his own was just one aspect of big-league life that he had never experienced before. Another was the abundance of free time he now had. And whom do single hockey players hang out with during their downtime but other single hockey players.

For better *and* for worse, Marcel was befriended by one of the team's genuine characters in Mickey Redmond. Not quite four years older than Marcel, Mickey was, like him, a young, talented forward with an incredible shot and one of the few bright spots on the Red Wings roster. Mickey was also both spirited and in possession of a keen understanding of the environment in which he lived. Being of like—and opinionated—minds, Marcel inevitably gravitated toward Redmond's company. "Mickey Redmond started to call me Moses," Marcel says. "He was a bad influence. Good guy, he's still a good friend of mine today, but Mickey was anti-management, anti-coach, anti-hockey, and you name it. He was everything you didn't want to be mixed up with. So I learned a lot from him."

Mickey Redmond responds: "I used to try to help out a lot of the younger players, and I'd have a lot of them live at my house; it's the same house I live in today. When they got called up they'd get two weeks' hotel [allowance] and then they'd be on their own, so I used to take a lot of young players in. They would come and go, and I don't recall even charging them rent, although they certainly had to pay their food-and-drink bill. These guys were in transit. I mean, what the heck, they're young guys, it's the end of the season—they couldn't buy houses. So, there were a number of guys that lived with us, two, three, four at a time.

"At first, I think Marcel was a little tentative to branch out when he arrived in Detroit. But after a couple of months I think he realized that that was what he needed to do, to be with the other guys. In junior, you went to school, you lived with a family, and it's just not the same business that hockey is at the NHL level. And it's not easy for people to adapt to life off the ice, especially because there is so much free time. You'd practise for an hour and a half or two hours a day, and the rest of the day is nothing. It's whatever. In those days, obviously, times were different. And you had *nothing* else to do."

Compared to the team commitments, schedules and outside business opportunities that players are tied up with today, the experience that Marcel met at the beginning of his NHL career marked the tail end of a different era in professional hockey. It wouldn't be long before Marcel Dionne would play a leading role in altering the standards for hockey players in this regard. But for the time being, he was being educated on the finer points of doing nothing.

"God, I don't know," Redmond ponders. "What did we do? I guess we just wasted a lot of time. We had a ton of time on our hands. And sometimes too much, which was not good for a young person. I know I had a hard time with it in Montreal. You can only go to see so many shows and things like that. Society has changed so much since the early '70s. Yeah, there were a lot of bad habits you could get into and you had to be careful not to get trapped by those things. Obviously a lot of guys did, but you have to learn to deal with that kind of stuff.

"The first few months with the team Marcel was getting comfortable with everybody. His language was a bit of a barrier at first, but in a short time he was able to converse back and forth with the guys. After a while I think he understood that living with other guys who were doing the same thing, who had the same in-and-out schedule, was the way to go."

While Mickey Redmond is cautiously reluctant to disclose the nitty-gritty of the NHL bachelor's daily routine, perhaps the most scandalous aspect was simply the staggering amount of time in which they actually *did* do nothing. In the case of the Detroit Red Wings, what Mickey had come to realize, and imparted to Marcel, was that if you're going to be doing nothing, you're much better off doing it with other people who had nothing to do.

As their friendship developed, the door at the Redmond home came to be open to Dionne on a round-the-clock basis. "Marcel used to come over to my house all of the time. I used to laugh about it because the bugger would come over, eat my food, read my newspaper, and then he'd throw the newspaper on the floor and leave. I think he was getting a taste of it before one day when he came to me and said, 'You know, Mick, I think that maybe it would be a good idea for me to come and live here.' I said, 'Whatever you want to do, Marcel.'" Although Dionne never actually moved into Mickey's house, Marcel's visits were frequent enough for Redmond to wonder whether he actually had.

———————

Given the many thrills that are part of every player's first NHL season, from playing in the legendary rinks to skating with the best in the game, there is little else on a rookie's mind outside of hockey. In Marcel's case, his preoccupation was beneficial; it allowed the time away from Carol to pass by rather quickly. However, such wasn't the case for Carol. Even prior to the season, she questioned whether their relationship could survive the time and distance apart. "The only fight we ever had was when Marcel was drafted to Detroit. I looked at the team's schedule to see how often he was going to play in Buffalo or Toronto, where I might get to see him. When I saw how infrequent that was, I said, 'That's it.' So I told him, 'Do whatever you want. If you meet a girl, go out with her. If I meet a guy, I'll go out with him.'" Needless to say, it pleased Carol to discover that Marcel was as devoted to her as he was to hockey.

Marcel still had Carol in his heart, but at the front of his mind were the daily lessons he was learning at work. If the introduction to the Red Wings organization at training camp had troubled Marcel, little that followed would alleviate those concerns. The club lacked sound leadership at the top, and that trickled down through the team, and out the door.

"The first year in the league you are so happy. You are excited to go to the Chicago Stadium, the Boston Garden, to Philadelphia; win or lose, you want to do your best. In the process, as a rookie, you look to the older players to carry the team. But in Detroit, suddenly those players were gone. From the day I arrived, they traded everybody; it was a constant revolving door. We had an owner who was a drunk. Bruce Norris would come into our dressing room drunk out of his mind. We had people that were not qualified—it's not that they were bad people, they just weren't qualified. So as a young player, I found that you couldn't look to someone else to carry the team. It was up to you! And that's okay, because that's what you are there for, but at the same time, it's nice to have certain players, the leaders, stay with the team."

Another cold reality that Marcel had to face in his first year in the NHL was the attention and criticism of the press. Although he had read articles about himself throughout his ascent to the NHL, a higher degree of scrutiny was going to be the standard from now on. The knock against Marcel, which was as much of a curse as it was a blessing in his career, was his body type. One would think that if an athlete gets the job done, his or her physique should not matter. However, regardless of common sense, it is also true that appearance is frequently a component of popularity. In the eyes of some, Marcel Dionne fell short on this count.

The upside to his physical stature, as far as hockey was concerned, was that his stocky build and low centre of gravity made the speedy forward difficult to catch or move off the puck. Those who considered Dionne in some way physically lacking would find their assessment invalidated in every single game that he played. And yet, despite his achievements and self-confidence, that perception of a downside left its mark.

"When I first came into Montreal to play the Canadiens, this guy wrote an article and targeted me right away. He wrote about me, stating that I had a pudgy stomach. Well, all my life I've had a little pudge there. Whether I weighed 165 pounds or 190, I've always had that. He then went on about me being overrated, that I was a little fat cat. I thought, 'Why is he picking on me?' But that's what reporters do. They're not satisfied unless you're the perfect physical specimen, so they criticize your body. I said, 'Well, I'm sorry, there's only about four billion of us in that category.' So you make the best with what you've got. It's not easy for guys of our stature. You are always told that you are too short. And big guys are told they are too tall. So what can you do?

"It never bothered me. Well, it bothered me in the sense that they make an issue of it. The terrible thing about it is that they forget there's a lot of young kids that have dreams. It's okay if they criticize me, but what they don't realize is the number of people out there in the same boat. You'd be amazed at the number of guys that have approached me and told me that they used to be Marcel Dionne. I laugh every time and say, 'Shit, you must have been a little runt.' But people don't know how tough it is. I know how tough it is—mentally tough. You have to be fearless. You put yourself in a position where you know you're going to get nailed.

And to survive, you have to find tricks. You have to be quicker, more aggressive and you can't give up. You have to let the opposition know that no matter how many times they hit you, you're still going to be there. Only then will you become less of a target. Eventually, they stop trying to intimidate you because they know it won't work. You're always aware of who the tough guys are, the guys who think they're tough when they give you a cheap shot. With those guys, you know it's coming, so you brace yourself."

To play in the NHL you simply had to have the sand. But to be the player that the opposition keyed in on every night, and survive—if not thrive—required something more. Dionne understood that to be successful he would have to be cocksure. And Marcel had no problem fitting the bill. It was a part that suited his character to the point of enjoying the role; in fact, he was so comfortable with it that he often took more abuse from his own teammates than he did from the opposition.

"They were always after me. I was a real yapper. I yapped all the time and challenged the guys. As a result, I didn't really enjoy going to practice because I didn't know if I'd be going home with clothes or not. They'd rip them, hide them, put talcum powder in my pockets. Or I'd stick my hand in my pocket looking for change and it would come out covered in Vaseline. They also used to nail your shoes to the floor.

"I remember I had this wool sweater, so they threw it in the whirlpool. I pulled it out and the thing had stretched like crazy. I thought, 'No problem, I'll just throw it in the dryer.' Well, I pulled it out, and for Chrissakes, it shrunk so badly it went from being too big to being too small. Our team did tricks like that all the time. They would cut your underwear; you'd put your socks on and see your toes. Everyday they would get my stuff. And it was a nightmare if you came in with something new because they'd be sure to get that."

Day-to-day pranks were enough to keep the players on their toes, but the formal initiation was another matter. Red Wings teammate Nick Libett recalled the standard practice around the league: "Our team wasn't unique in this manner. I think all of the teams did it. Nowadays you'd probably get put in jail because what it amounted to was assault and battery. Basically, there was a shaving ritual where you would shave the pubic area, that's number one, and with Marcel we took it from there."

Marcel adds: "Because I was so vocal and loved to have fun, right off the bat they had me in their sights, no doubt about it. So it was just a matter of time before they would initiate me. One day at practice our goalie, Al Smith, came and sat beside me, wanting me to look at an article in the newspaper. Man, did I get sucked in. They sit next to you so they can grab a hold of you because nobody wants to take a punch. So I didn't see it coming. I said to Al, 'Oh, yeah, what's in the article?' Then they all grabbed me and I said, 'Oh shit.' And they're big guys, so what can you do? I fought and screamed and told them that I was going to kill every one of them. They had a bucket of water, and when I opened my mouth they'd pour water down my throat. I thought I was going to drown. The entire time, you're blindfolded so you can't see who is doing what. Next came the hot water they dribbled on me, and they were shouting, 'Uhh, someone is peeing on you!' So then I'm screaming and yelling and they sprayed shaving cream into my mouth. And the more you fight, the worse they give it to you, hitting you in the stomach. I swear to God, I thought I was going to die.

"Through this process, basically what they are doing is giving you the razor and shaving you. Well, in those days everybody was growing sideburns. On top of everything they did to me, they had to cut my sideburns. So now what happens is we have a game that night and we're going on the road. Of course, I'm thinking of how I can get even with them. And when they let go of me, I said, 'I'm gonna get even with every last one of you.' And you know they've heard that before, but you've got to say something. So what I did was, I went to a barbershop and I had the barber fix me up with false sideburns.

"Later that afternoon we're at the airport getting on the plane, and Mickey Redmond is looking at me and I'm not saying a word. He realizes that something isn't quite right but he can't put his finger on what it is. He says, 'There's something wrong, you look different.' Just as he's asking the other guys on the team what looks strange, he shouts, 'He's got *false sideburns!*' Then Mickey tackles me in the airport and he's trying to pull the sideburns off, but he can't because they're glued on. So we played the game that night, I believe it was in Minnesota. Well, the whole time I'm thinking about the sideburns, hoping that they're staying on straight. I was worried that I'd get hit on the ice and come up with crooked sideburns. I took them off after that one game; it was my way of getting back at them."

Chapter Five

IN MARCEL'S FIRST SEASON with the Detroit Red Wings he played centre, predominantly between Nick Libett and Bill Collins. The pairing with Libett in particular complemented Dionne the rookie, who benefited from his steady play and rugged support. "It was great to play with Nick," Marcel recalls. "Nick was a give-and-go, straight-up-and-down player, and I think we really enjoyed playing on the same line. It was good for me because he didn't mind getting involved and taking guys on when it was called for. I remember he stepped in a few times on my behalf; I appreciated that very much. Plus, he had me over to his house a few times for dinner. As a matter of fact, after everybody got traded, Nick was the only guy that remained in Detroit; he went on to play eleven years with the Red Wings. It's amazing—Nick was the only guy that Ned Harkness kept."

Libett offers an amusing assessment of his staying power in Detroit. "I look back and think, either nobody wanted me or I was too valuable to the team to trade—and I don't think either of those statements is true. In those days, every year we anticipated a good season at the start, but things in the mid '70s just seemed to go south because we just didn't have the eighteen quality players, or the one superstar like Marcel that you could form your team around."

Throughout his first season, Marcel showed that he was indeed the type of franchise player Detroit needed to build around. Amongst such seasoned pros as Alex Delvecchio, Red Berenson and Mickey Redmond, he led the team in scoring with 77 points, followed by Redmond's 71; Dionne's impressive total set a new league record for points by a rookie.

One might think such an accomplishment would stand him in

good stead for rookie of the year honours, but the Calder Trophy escaped not only his grasp, but that of the player Marcel had pegged for the award. "The guy that should have won the rookie of the year was Rick Martin; he scored 44 goals in his first NHL season. They gave it to Kenny Dryden. You're gonna tell me it's not political? I'm happy for Ken, but I'll tell you, if you ask me, Rick Martin was the guy." As a new franchise, Martin's Buffalo Sabres didn't have the clout that the Montreal Canadiens had, nor did Martin have the Stanley Cup that Dryden had earned in such spectacular fashion the previous spring. The voters favoured the proven winner.

Calder Trophy or not, Dionne's rookie season proved to the Detroit organization that he was the real deal; and perhaps more importantly, he had made a leap forward in building his own confidence. Dionne believed this would help him lead the Red Wings to where they wanted to be in the standings in 1972–73, though it was going to be a long, hard road.

Marcel's rookie year was diametrically opposed to that of Guy Lafleur in Montreal. While Marcel enjoyed the fact that his playing time enabled him to make all of the incentives in his first-year contract (more than doubling his $18,000 salary), Lafleur's team was in the playoffs; the Wings were not. "Guy was in a better environment, but he was having a tougher time getting to play. I managed to play, but I was in a bad environment. Sure, we had fun, but where are we going? What's our purpose? Are we going to win?"

Gearing up for his second season, Marcel hoped to move the Red Wings in that very direction. First, however, he would find himself presented with a unique opportunity to further his hockey education. "For me, in my second season, everything took off. I was up there in scoring with Espo and Orr. I scored 40 goals— I could have scored about 100. Why did I have such a great year? I went to camp with Team Canada '72, my greatest experience of all time."

While Dionne was hasty to point out that hockey politics had, in his opinion, given Ken Dryden the Calder, he was equally swift in qualifying his presence on Team Canada. "The only reason I was picked for that team was Alan Eagleson [Marcel's agent, who did double duty as the czar of Team Canada and made sure that players he represented dominated the roster of high-profile names]. There's no other way I could have been on that team."

Whereas an NHL team dresses twenty players for each game, the organizers of Team Canada invited a whopping thirty-five to attend training camp at Toronto's Maple Leaf Gardens in August.

"It was the first format ever for that type of series, so now I am able to see and understand why it was done the way it was," Marcel says. "They had to pick a lot of players for the training camp. I had just finished my rookie year, so Perreault, myself, the young guys, we came to camp flying. When you're twenty-one years old, you're in better shape than some of the twenty-seven- and twenty-eight-year-old guys. Back in those days, guys weren't in top shape after the summer. The reason for training camp in our day was to come and get in shape at training camp. I'm sorry, but that's the way it was. Training camp was a month. Guys would come overweight; they'd lose the weight and *boom*, they're ready to go. Today, that's not acceptable.

"So we went to camp and we were flying. The method of the training camp itself was that you were amongst the best players and you would be on the blue team or the red team or whatever, and you would play against each other. This continued up to the point when it was decided what the lineup was going to be."

As one of the younger players invited to camp, Dionne was attentive to every aspect of what was going on. He wanted to soak up every nuance of what he sensed was history in the making. Like most Canadian observers, he didn't know what to expect from the Russians. Looking back, he surmised that the Canadian brain trust running the show didn't know, either. "I don't think anybody knew how serious that series was going to be. In my opinion, even with the scouting reports we had, nobody knew what we were up against until we played that first game."

Unlike many of the veteran players, who appeared to be preoccupied with personal business, Marcel's sole focus was on playing hard and being ready to answer the call. "To this day people tell me that Harry Sinden is the greatest guy in the world. But those coaches didn't know what they were doing," Dionne states. "There we were at training camp, and we had players actually leaving to go and run their hockey schools. Guys were coming and going everywhere. I was saying, 'Holy shit, where are these guys going?'

"Then there was Bobby Orr, again a political thing. I remember being at practice, standing next to Serge Savard, and Bobby was skating. Well, he had just come off of surgery. I asked Serge, 'What is he doing here?' Serge said, 'He's only here for the hype. They're trying to get some publicity for this thing. Jesus, just look at the guy; he's hurting. He can't play.' Serge wasn't saying anything bad about Bobby, it was just part of what was going on surrounding the series."

Once the team's final roster was set, and prior to the series' opening game, Team Canada enjoyed a day of golf at the Lambton Golf & Country Club in Toronto. The intent of the excursion was twofold: to allow the team to relax, and to let those unfamiliar with one another get a little time in away from the rink. Being one of the greener players, Marcel was pleased to socialize with the league's elite and participate in a casual round of golf. Of the players he got better acquainted with that day, Peter Mahovlich remains one of Marcel's favourite golfing buddies.

According to Mahovlich, "Marcel had a lot of enthusiasm. He was a real team guy. He's not a big man height-wise, but he certainly played big. I mean, *strong* on his skates; he had good quickness, and it was very difficult to get the puck off of him down low. Of course, he didn't have a lot of support in Detroit and then he went to Los Angeles. Again, there wasn't much support for him there. Consequently, he didn't get to achieve what he really wanted, which was to play on a Stanley Cup team. So I think he really embraced part of that '72 series because of the fact that we were able to win.

"I can remember that day we went to golf, and Dale Tallon and

I were getting ready to play. Dale, when he was fifteen or sixteen, was the Canadian junior golf champion—I mean, he was a great amateur golfer, and I had been playing for quite some time and was about a five or six handicap. So we were looking to get guys in our foursome who could really play. Marcel had just taken up the game and wanted to come out and play with us. And we tried to be as polite as possible, but we told him, 'No, we want to have a real serious game.' So Marcel was told to take his clubs and go play somewhere else."

For Marcel, the snub on the golf course led to one of many lessons he would learn over the course of the '72 series. "I don't know who put the foursomes together, but I was put in a group with Pete Mahovlich and Dale Tallon. I guess they assumed I played golf. I was twenty-one years old and was just happy to be with these guys. Well, Dale Tallon is a scratch golfer and Pete is about a five handicap. After I hit my third ball those frickin' guys gassed me. 'F— off, get lost!' So you know what I did? I said, 'Okay, I will remember this day.' Pete and I play a lot of golf together, and Pete loves to gamble. So last summer I kicked his ass bad. He gets money off of me, too, but you know what I learned about life? I thought it was just okay to play golf. Well, it's not okay. If you're going to play, you had better learn about the game. So I went back and learned how to play the game. That was my first lesson with those guys.

"The second lesson I learned was when I opened my mouth about my wife-to-be. I knew this series was history in the making. I didn't know how big a part of history it was going to be, but I've always shared the important things in my life with the people who are close to me, and Carol was the person who was closest to me. So I asked her mom and told her that this could be an incredible opportunity. Then I asked Gilbert Perreault, 'Why don't you bring your girlfriend?' And that was considered taboo then, but I felt that was irrelevant because of the opportunity before us. I believe I was the only player to bring a girlfriend. And if you ask Carol today, she will tell you that the trip to Russia was one of the greatest experiences of her life. So the day of that golf tournament there was a discussion about players taking their wives. And I mentioned that, if it were possible, I would like to take my girl-friend. Well, that was all it took for Eagleson. Al answered real quick and started making fun of it. He said, 'You're not going to believe this one—Dionne wants to bring his girlfriend!' He thought it was funny. But I was hurt by that. I thought, 'Son of a bitch! You can't keep anybody's mouth shut.' And now I'm still married to Carol, and most of those guys are divorced, so I haven't done too bad."

Part of the logic behind having young players on the roster was that it was a lot easier on the coaching staff to sideline them than to bench one of the All-Stars who expected to play. From the start, Team Canada's strategy was to go with the veterans, and rightly so. However, this did little to diminish Dionne's desire to help the team, especially after witnessing Team Canada's sluggish per-formance in Russia's 7–3 onslaught in game one.

"After the first game, I walked into our dressing room and went over to Yvan Cournoyer. Most of the guys still had their jerseys on, and did they ever look tired. Yvan said to me, 'Marcel, they are unbelievable. They are so strong.' If that is coming from one of the fastest players that has ever played the game, the Roadrunner, I thought, holy shit.

"Now, when he said that to me, I'm eager to play. I'm thinking, 'Man, I want to get in that lineup; I'll skate so fast.' I was just dying [to play]. And we had the speed. But that's where the expe-rience plays a big part and makes the difference. You've got to have experience. But I wish I could have played just one shift with Gilbert Perreault to show that we could skate, too. Then again, how can you replace the other guys? The coaches made the decision to go with experience. That's how Harry Sinden covered himself. He's never been one of my favourite guys, but he had to do what he had to do. You have to respect that, and understand it."

For game two in Toronto, the coaching staff of Harry Sinden and John Ferguson tweaked the Team Canada roster, benching finesse players like Jean Ratelle and Rod Gilbert in favour of more physical skaters, such as Wayne Cashman and Pat Stapleton. Although the lineup changes didn't satisfy Dionne's desire to play, he couldn't argue with the result on the ice. "We went back to Toronto, where we all witnessed one of the greatest goals of all time."

In the third period, with Canada clinging to a 2–1 lead, Stapleton took a minor penalty. While killing the penalty up front with Phil Esposito, Peter Mahovlich was able to gather a clearing pass and turn up ice. Quickly meeting the lone defender at the Soviet blue line, Mahovlich wound up but opted to fake his shot, allowing him to deke by. With only Vladislav Tretiak standing between him and the goal, big Pete barrelled in and, at the last possible second, put on the brakes and stuck a backhand past the Russian goalie, leaving him draped over the net. The short-handed work of art was crucial in Canada's 4–1 victory and had everyone in Maple Leaf Gardens, including an impressed Marcel Dionne, cheering their approval. "When Pete Mahovlich scored that goal, to me, that was just the most spectacular goal that I've ever seen.

"So the second game went by and I'm dying to get in the lineup. Well, we won the game, but now I know there's no chance for me. Then it was on to Winnipeg, where we tied [4–4]. I'm still dying. Then it became really tough. For those of us that didn't get to play, that was very hard."

As one of the inexperienced members of the team, Dionne's psyche would have benefited from an explanation of what the coaching staff had in mind for the younger players. Even if it meant more of the same, waiting and preparing for their number to be called, a definite signal would have been better than what they received. "I'll tell you," Dionne fumes, "there was no communication. All they had to do was say, 'Here's what your status is.' It wasn't so much John Ferguson—John was all right—but Harry Sinden. Harry Sinden had no communication skills whatsoever.

"The players were phenomenal with their support. You see, when you don't play—and I understand this, having played all of my life—when you have guys that don't play, they hang around and you feel for them. But whether they are there or not makes absolutely no difference to those who are playing. Players know that. You feel for the guy that doesn't play—but guess what? You've got a game to play. The more you remove yourself from it, the better off the team is, because there's always that tension there. The other players who are playing understand this, and that's all you want, the mutual respect."

With the series tied heading into the fourth game, Team Canada felt the heat for not being ahead in the series. Not only was the press sticking it to the Canadian squad, but the fans in the host city of Vancouver really let the home team have it. During the game, which was dominated by Team Russia in a 5–3 win, the efforts of Team Canada were met with a chorus of boos. At the conclusion of another disappointing outcome, Phil Esposito, on national television, responded to the ill will shown to the Canadian players. "To people across Canada, we're trying our best . . . we came because we love Canada . . . I don't think it's fair that we should be booed."

The interview that Esposito gave might seem tame by today's standards; however, people at the time were shocked that a professional athlete would lash back at the public, censuring fans for knocking their efforts. Ultimately, the disrespect and criticism that Esposito had damned in his interview would be tacked onto the list of grievances that, in turn, served to strengthen the team's resolve to win.

Indeed, many intriguing stories were born from the 1972 Canada–Russia series. Of the many subplots that evolved within these stories, the one that was closest to Marcel Dionne's experience was that of the players who returned to Canada from Russia before the series was over: Gilbert Perreault, Rick Martin, Jocelyn Guevremont and Vic Hadfield. Considering the circumstances of these players, who had been more or less shelved for the series, their desire to address matters in their own lives was entirely reasonable. Unknowingly and undeservedly, they were in turn vilified in the press by Harry Sinden for their decision to leave. Although Marcel did not return to Canada, he just as easily could have.

"There's two sides to that story," Dionne battles. "I'll meet anyone's challenge who says those guys quit on the team. They didn't quit on the team. Vic Hadfield may have been a different case. He had experience the younger guys didn't have and might have known better, but somebody should have grabbed him and explained why he should stay. If he had known the consequences that he had to face later on—and Vic is a good friend of mine— I'm sure he would have thought twice about it before he left. These guys became traitors in the press and the public eye, but I was no different from them; I could have left for home. It came to the point where you asked yourself, 'Should I go back home? They've got enough guys here.' And I was thinking this way because it was never explained to me that you've got to stay until the end. No one said, 'Here's what the commitment is, this is what's at stake.' I've always felt sorry for those guys who left, because I could have been right there with them. I don't know why I didn't go home.

"You have to understand, as a player you have so much energy, and if you're not able to play, it eats away at you. Now, it's easy for me to look back on and talk about, and I'm happy with the way things turned out. Although I didn't get to play against Russia, I got to play two exhibition games, one in Sweden and one in Czechoslovakia. But to be there and to be part of that team, it was the greatest time of my life. It was the history of it more than the game itself. It was the value of what took place. A free country versus a system that we didn't understand."

Before the series resumed in Moscow, Team Canada visited

Sweden and played two games against that country's best. The layover in Sweden was intended to be a preparation for the four games against Russia—a chance to adjust to the larger ice surface and to the time change. For the charged-up Dionne, settling down to rest was impossible. "Pat Stapleton was my roommate. He was a beauty. He always called me 'Kid.' And he always locked me out of our room. If I wasn't in the room on time—and the reason didn't matter—I couldn't get in. For the first three days in Europe, I was a mess. Emotionally I was a mess. All of these veterans were able to go to sleep, but that would be the time when I'd be waking up. Then they would wake up and I would be going to bed. It was really hard for me, and at the time I didn't know why. I would try to go to sleep, but you see, I wasn't a drinker. I was twenty-one years old and I didn't know how to adjust. Some of the veterans would simply have a few pops, so for them relaxing and adjusting wasn't a problem."

In addition to his body clock being off, as a younger player, Marcel couldn't fully appreciate the burden the veteran players were carrying. After the passionate speech made by Phil Esposito after the loss in Vancouver, the entire country felt the tension surrounding the series. But to witness up close the way that various players on the team coped with the situation served only to heighten Dionne's distress.

It was in Sweden that he voiced his concern to team leader Phil Esposito. "I was with Phil one night and we were eating at the hotel. I said to him, 'You know what, these Russians are going to beat us.' So Phil turns around, and you know Phil, '*What* are you talking about? *How* can you say that? *What* gives you the right to say that?!' "

Having played the Russians, Esposito would undoubtedly have a better feel for Canada's chances; nevertheless, his scolding did little to relieve his understudy's concerns. From the comings and goings at the ill-prepared training camp to the social events in Sweden, Dionne had yet to see the serious approach to the series that he had assumed Team Canada would have displayed throughout. The pinnacle of distraction came one night in Stockholm's red-light district, where a contingent of the team and members of the Canadian press took in some live entertainment.

"We went to this place, Le Chat Noir," confesses Dionne. "I had never been exposed to a place that had a prostitute district. So we went there, and the Canadian press was there—like *they* had never been to that sort of establishment before—and we all watched live sex on stage. I'm thinking to myself, 'Holy shit.' Then a couple of our players got up on stage and dropped their pants! It was all in fun; nothing dirty happened. All the guys were laughing. But from my perspective, I'm thinking, this is crazy. We're supposed to be playing hockey."

Whatever was on the team's itinerary and social agenda, the younger players were intent on making the scene. If nothing else, the trip was a once-in-a-lifetime event and they wanted to experience it fully. "We didn't want to miss a beat, we didn't want to miss anything. This was *the* thing to be involved in. But for a guy who has been around the league for ten years, well, he's been around. So things like the drinking weren't a big deal. I thought our drinking was really excessive. And I'm no saint, either, but I couldn't keep up with these guys. For some of the veterans it was, 'Ahh, kid, don't worry about it. F— it, so what, there's always tomorrow.' But I couldn't afford that attitude, being one of the young guys. There were players that were so drunk it was embarrassing. So frickin' drunk—every practice! It wasn't *all* the guys, but some of our players were under tremendous stress."

While this may come as a bit of a surprise, one must consider the cumulative stress factors the players were labouring under. Canada had fallen behind in the series against the Soviet National Team, a lesser rival they should have dominated. Smug expectations for victory had turned to mass ridicule from the entire country. The two exhibition games in Sweden turned out to be a pair of nasty and violent affairs that garnered more bad press. And last but not least, there was the uncertainty of what lay ahead in Moscow in the midst of what was a very real Cold War.

So, while the recreational activity in Sweden may have seemed untimely, if not inappropriate, it is understandable that Team Canada needed to blow off some steam. It's also conceivable that an element of the team's indiscreet behaviour could be attributed to the fact that this was a team of Canadian hockey players playing exhibition games in Europe on their vacation.

In Moscow, the members of Team Canada would collect themselves and address each of the remaining games with a determination that has not been equalled in the history of hockey. What made the difference that allowed for the storybook ending? According to Marcel, the arrival of the wives.

"The wives played a huge role. We left Sweden and headed to Russia, and that's where the wives joined us—and Carol, who was my girlfriend at the time, came too. After they arrived, everything was totally different. I couldn't believe the change that I witnessed. It was almost like every guy had woken up and said, 'Okay, now we're going to work.' It was incredible.

"In my opinion, every time a man is under stress or under pressure, who is his best partner? Who does he turn to? It's his wife. It seemed to me that at that point everybody calmed down. Suddenly, all the guys' minds were focused, they had a reason to get up, go to practice, come back and be with their wives. At training camp it was never taken seriously."

Once the second half of the series got under way in Russia, Dionne's excruciating desire to compete drove him to a new level of frustration. He and the other remaining extra players were relegated to practise on their own, separate from those who were seeing action in games. In a brief instance where his dissatisfaction got the best of him, Marcel opted to skip one such practice.

"When I was in Russia, around the second game, it started to drag. Between the month at training camp and the time it took for the series to play out, it was getting on seven weeks. It felt like there was no end to it. We'd get up in the morning and we were practising with just four guys. There was Eddie Johnston, myself, Brian Glennie and Dale Tallon. Mickey Redmond wasn't playing much because he had a sore back, and by this time Rick Martin, Jocelyn Guevremont, Gilbert Perreault and Vic Hadfield had left.

"One morning I woke up and said, 'I've had enough, too.' I didn't show up for practice because I just had nothing; I had no motivation to practise. I thought, 'I'm going home, I can't take this. It's killing me.' Shortly after, I saw Yvan Cournoyer and spoke to him. He knew what happened and settled me down. He said, 'Hey, Marcel, I understand. That's good, don't worry about it.' That made me feel better and got me on the right track. The entire incident lasted about an hour, and I was back to being happy to be there. If you care, you're going to have those moments. You can't accept a situation in which you have no purpose. It's the greatest series of all time; you want to contribute.

"Through that time I was fortunate. Eagleson was also there so I had Al to talk to as well. And that was the difference for me, having somebody to talk to. That's why I will never condemn the players who did go home. I don't care what Harry Sinden said; he didn't give a shit. He had no heart. When we were playing in Sweden, somebody on the team was injured and I went up to Harry and said, 'Harry, I will do anything to get in that lineup.' But certain coaches have biases against certain players, and you detect it right away. Even after the '72 series, when I went to Los Angeles, he condemned me for making all of that money. In the meantime he's making a million, and that's okay for him, but it's not okay for me? I never trusted that guy.

"I know the coaches had a difficult job having to cater to a lot of great players; I fully understand that. And I'm sure a lot of different players approached him, asking for a lot of different things. But his condemning the players that went home from Russia was wrong—saying those guys were traitors. And I read the articles that were going back home. But when Gilbert asked Harry about returning home, Harry told him that it wasn't a problem, that everything was fine. Then Harry told the press that the players quit on them. All he had to say to protect the players was that they understandably have things to do and that's okay. One philosophy is that because these guys are pros, they should know what to do. Well, these guys didn't know what the consequences would be. And they had to live with that decision for many years. I think to this day Gilbert and Rick regret that experience. Especially with Gilbert, it took a toll, absolutely. We've talked about it and it's not a pleasant subject. Gilbert was told that everything was okay, and Gilbert Perreault is as kind and as honest a human being as you'll ever meet. He said when they got off the plane they couldn't believe the press that was there, calling them traitors."

Despite the unpleasantness that was part of going to Russia in the midst of the Cold War—being under KGB surveillance, having their rooms bugged and food confiscated—Dionne and the rest of Team Canada found satisfaction in the end result. While all had assumed that Canada would have little difficulty walking over their opponents, Team Russia proved that it was indeed a worthy adversary. After losing 5–4 in the first of four games in Moscow, Team Canada displayed unmatched resilience in rallying to win the next three games *and* the series. This remarkable feat was highlighted by three consecutive game-winning goals by Paul Henderson. It stands as the greatest triumph in hockey history.

As much as the series is fondly remembered for the stellar performances of Paul Henderson and Phil Esposito, there were low points; at the top of the minus column was the dark cloud of media-fuelled hype that hung over the series every step of the way. Out of this, an inflated national responsibility was assigned to Team Canada. In turn, the criticism of the players' handling of that responsibility had a memorable effect on the players. Evidence of this came in the passionate monologue Esposito offered after the loss in Vancouver. Forced to be a spectator rather than an active participant, Dionne had the privilege to observe, from the eye of the hurricane, what amounted to a test of the human spirit. Through adverse conditions, under intense scrutiny, Team Canada prevailed.

"At the end of the day, there is one thing that the people following the series did not know, and that is what I learned from the experience of the Canada–Russia Series in '72. When the door on that room was shut, those twenty players, they're the ones that made the difference. They didn't care about the press, nor did it have anything to do with the fans, who gave us great support upon our return. It was those guys in that room that made the difference. That's all that matters to me—and I witnessed that."

Chapter Six

WITH THE CONCLUSION of his duties overseas, Dionne returned to the Detroit Red Wings for his second season in the NHL. Having been through the Team Canada training camp and having practised throughout the series, he was primed and ready for the NHL schedule. To his amazement, he noticed a distinct difference in the game. "From the day I put on my skates at the Team Canada training camp it was high tempo all the way. Because we were amongst all of the elite players in the NHL our intrasquad games were played at an extremely fast pace.

"When I walked into the Detroit training camp and got on the ice, everything in front of me appeared to be in slow motion. It was absolutely incredible how the rate just dropped. Then our season began, and that feeling stayed with me. I saw the game as if it was moving in slow motion. I was in this zone, and it remained that way for the entire season. I think nearly everybody returning from the '72 series had good years. Gilbert Perreault had a great year, Bobby Clarke just blossomed, Ron Ellis, Paul Henderson, Gary Bergman was outstanding, Kenny Dryden—the Montreal Canadiens won the Cup. So everybody who was part of Team Canada '72 benefited from the experience in their careers."

In his second year with the Detroit Red Wings, Marcel tallied an impressive 40 goals and 50 assists for 90 points. But while he was motoring through the schedule, the overall picture for the team wasn't as promising. The losses piled up, and management showed little ability to correct the situation. In the midst of one losing skid, coach Johnny Wilson tried in vain to motivate his players.

"It was in my second year. We came back from a road trip and we had a practice the following morning. I think we had returned from Minnesota, so everybody was tired. The [players] thought we were going to go home, but they called a practice. It was a Sunday morning, and we had a game that evening. So we're at this practice and we're skating and Johnny Wilson is screaming at some of the older guys on the team, players whom I have a great deal of respect for. He shouted, 'If anybody doesn't feel good about this practice, you can leave the ice right now!' Well, that's all I needed to hear, so I left.

"That's been in my character over the years. If you're going to say something, you had better back it up. We had guys that would never challenge that sort of treatment. I thought, 'All right, you said we could leave, let's see what's going to happen. If you want us at practice, don't tell us we can leave.' I mean, why even say that? All of your life you hear that through junior, and now you turn pro and you hear the same bullshit. I thought that would change. I was so excited to be at that next level where I expected it to be different, but it was the same thing all over again—team punishment. It was on a Sunday, and there was a game that evening and I never showed up.

"I think they suspended me, and I said, 'Fine, suspend me,' because there's a side of me that is very stubborn. When it comes to that point, if you want to challenge me, I'll take the challenge. But in that situation I was wrong in leaving, and I know I was wrong. I was just trying to make a point that they shouldn't challenge certain people simply because they have the power. You're supposed to sit there like a fool and take it. I felt somebody should stand up and say, 'Hold on, here's what we've got to do, we're all in it together,' and help us understand what we need to work on rather than putting people down. I want to play here. I want to do well. But you get tired of losing, and my walkout was a reaction to what had been building up inside of me."

Conspicuous by his absence, the press reported that Dionne was missing for no apparent reason and nobody seemed to know why. To sort out what had become an awkward situation, a sound voice of reason intervened. "Gordie Howe called me," Dionne starts with a smile. " 'Beaver,' he said—Gordie called me Beaver—'What's going on?' He was just great, but I had difficulty expressing myself to Gordie as well. He basically said, 'You know what? I played for Jack Adams, and not every day was a great day, and I had my run-ins with him.' Then he told me to just let it blow over and get right back into the thick of things. I thought, 'Wow, coming from Gordie Howe, that's good enough for me.' That phone call meant a lot. So it was resolved within a day, and the next game I was back with the team."

Dionne acknowledged that his frustration with the Detroit organization was mistakenly directed at Johnny Wilson. Unfortunately, decisions made above the coach's head left a once-powerful team in a dilapidated state. The downward spiral that had begun prior to Dionne's arrival seemed nowhere near being corrected under the management of Ned Harkness.

Having enjoyed the game of hockey his entire life, Dionne was shocked to discover how quickly that could change. "I just didn't understand it. It never happened in junior. I played for some good teams and it was always fun to play. All of a sudden, it was no longer fun; it became a serious business. Later in your career you understand that every game, every shift means so much because it's big money at stake. I just didn't understand that. I thought there would be some compassion, but I would see guys getting shipped out all the time. From the day I arrived in Detroit I must have played with a hundred different guys. Where's your sense of security when you see that kind of turnover?

"You're with your friends one day, the next day they're gone and another group comes in. It leaves you confused. So you start to put up a wall. Some players don't understand that. New players come in and you know them, but you don't want to get to know them too well because they could be gone the next day, and it hurts you. It's not unusual to have a trade here and there, but six or seven guys . . . I mean, every training camp most of the guys would be gone. So you put up a fence. Initially, a lot of players don't understand that, until one day they find out for themselves that that's how it works."

In Marcel's rookie season, he had seen the organization's capacity for cold treatment at its zenith. Gordie Howe had retired the year before his arrival, and the Red Wings felt that in Marcel they had landed a franchise player who could accept and carry the torch. While Dionne aspired to fit the bill, the transition would have been that much smoother with Howe's guidance. Sadly, Dionne learned that even the greatest player in the game had no tenure with the management of the day.

"In my first year, Gordie was still around the team. I don't know that he had been given a title yet, but he was taking practice with us. So Gordie comes on the ice and he's in a sweatsuit, shooting on the goalies. I'm thinking 'Holy shit, this is great.' Well, doesn't Harkness come along and tell him to get out of here. He didn't want him around. And I never saw him at practice again. Can you imagine that? When I saw them do that to Mr. Hockey, I thought, 'Well, who am I to them? If they're doing that to Gordie Howe, what kind of treatment will *I* get?' So I always kept that incident in the back of my mind when I negotiated a contract or considered a fresh start. The bottom line is, you've got to look after yourself.

"Imagine Gordie Howe saying, 'Marcel, here's what you should be doing,' this and that. My God, I've never had a teacher before, now I've got one. It would have been the ideal thing to have Gordie there, not only for me, and not so much for the older guys, but for all the young players. And I think Gordie might have liked to do that because he just got out of playing and hadn't decided what he was going to pursue."

Although Dionne didn't receive the tutelage he first envisioned, many of the veterans did serve as mentors for the younger players. As is the custom with all hockey teams, rookies were paired with veterans on road trips. Three of Dionne's roommates in the early years were Red Berenson, Gary Bergman and Alex Delvecchio. Dionne remembers each with respect and admiration. "I remember rooming with Red Berenson in Buffalo. He was a real outdoorsman; he loved hunting and fishing. I always respected him as a player—quite strong, and a quiet person. So we're in Buffalo and it's really cold outside. I returned to our room in time for cur-few, opened the door, and it was freezing in our room. I walked in; Red was asleep in bed, he's wearing a toque and the window is wide open. Well, there must have been a foot of snow piled up on the floor by the window. I said, 'What the hell is going on?' I looked at him and he started to laugh and went right back to sleep. He liked the cold weather.

"Gary Bergman was my point man. One night in Toronto, Johnny Wilson put me on the right point with him on a power play; after that, we played the point together on all of the power plays. He didn't have a shot, so he always fed me the puck. That was a case [where] sometimes you don't appreciate a player until you lose him or need him. I enjoyed Gary very much. He was Alex Delvecchio's buddy; a one-two combination, and they sat at the back of the bus together. I remember an experience with Gary that made me reflect on the fact that when you're a kid you're learning about life, and basically you're happy all day long. This one evening I was rooming with Gary, and he received a phone call. It was his wife, and she told him that she had been diagnosed with some kind of cancer—she's still alive today. But I was listen-ing because I couldn't ignore the conversation. After the phone call, I was so nervous, I was in shock, I said, 'Oh, my God' and I felt so bad for him. And that's a part of the life that hockey fans never see. They see the performance on the ice but they don't know that, two hours prior to the game, the player has learned that his wife has cancer. And now that player has to perform. So, later on in my career I had a rule with Carol and my family to never call me on the road, unless it was an emergency. Don't call me, I'll call you.

"With Alex Delvecchio . . . Christ, Alex had twenty years' experi-ence on me, silver-grey hair—he could have been my dad. I remem-ber watching him skate—ahh, geez, he was just a beautiful skater. When I roomed with Alex I was in awe. I'll never forget Alex getting ready for bed. It was funny to me, because he'd wear these really nice pyjamas and he would put his hair in a hairnet, over his head like a lady would, so when he would get up in the morning his hair would be nice and neat. To be roommates with these guys—you couldn't enjoy it because you were just petrified. But Alex, Gary and Red, they were my three favourite roommates."

By Dionne's third season with the Red Wings he had graduated from a veteran roommate to a more contemporary pairing with Mickey Redmond. Since he had enjoyed countless hours of downtime at Mickey's house, Dionne knew what to expect. While he wasn't as awe-inspiring as Alex Delvecchio, Redmond had always been an admirable person to Marcel. "Mickey was totally different from the other players on the team. When I had Mickey for a roommate on the road, he'd always come in late. I would be sleeping, and there would be this noise; it was a mouth chomping loudly. I would turn over and there would be Mickey, eating a big hamburger at the side of his bed, stinking up the room. He'd always come in with these late-night snacks. And he would say between bites, 'Hey, midget, do you want some?' He always called me names. I would say, 'No way do I want any!' He drove me nuts, but you get to appreciate all of your roommates. We had a lot of good times. I had more laughs with the guys in Detroit, which was definitely a different situation from playing in California. When you play in California, you spend so much time travelling and commuting that you simply don't have the same amount of free time for the fun stuff.

"When I played with the Red Wings, because travel was light, we were always going out to different places or having dinner at a restaurant after a game. Then you would return to your hotel room and a couple of guys would be waiting in your room to plow you with a bucket of water when you opened the door. It was crazy, and there was no end to it. It was like a bunch of kids—and that's what it should be—having fun together."

Although the good times were memorable, what stands out in Dionne's mind from his third season was a frustrating scoring drought, the likes of which he had never experienced before. From the outset of the season, he went twenty-one games without scoring a single goal. "I remember one time they put me out there when the opposing team pulled their goalie, just so I could get an empty-netter to get me out of my slump. So I got the puck and shot it down the ice. It hit the post."

While he wondered how he could alter the course of his bad luck, Dionne's persistent work ethic on the ice won the support of fans who lifted his spirits with letters of encouragement and advice. One suggested that he formally change his name to O'Dionne to evoke the luck of the Irish. Eventually, his season got on track and he finished the year with 24 goals and 54 assists.

While Marcel set about salvaging his year, Mickey Redmond had cruised to his second fifty-goal season in a row. No Red Wing had ever before netted 50, and now Redmond had done it twice. With his talent as a sniper and Dionne's promise as a marquee player, there should have been plenty of cause for optimism in the Red Wings dressing room. However, Dionne recalls a team meeting, held around the time of his scoring slump, that revealed a chink in the team's chemistry. Marcel knew he had not delivered up to that point, but when he saw his teammates harp on the efforts of Mickey Redmond, who *was* producing, he was further discouraged. Although Marcel never had a problem with Mickey's role, he could see that other players did.

"Mickey practised at his own pace, and some of the guys didn't like that. I remember this meeting we had, and the entire meeting became, 'Mickey should be doing this' and 'Mickey should be doing that.' Then they were saying, 'Look how hard Marcel is working.' And Mickey was pissed off; you see, he was the type of guy who got under the skin of some guys. Personally, I loved every minute of what he did. I knew him and understood him. But some of the players didn't like his work ethic. Well, the guy had two fifty-goal seasons, and they weren't happy with that. I don't give a shit if he was a one-way player. Who cares? He scored 50 goals!

"When we had that meeting everybody was talking and I was sitting thinking, 'These guys are down on Mickey and I haven't scored in almost twenty games.' That was wrong. The reason for a team meeting is to clear the air; instead it all ended up on Mickey's shoulders. But Mickey wasn't a leader. He did it on the ice.

"Mickey was a bull. People don't realize the strength this guy had. The team didn't care for his work ethic, or his anti-management views, but he sure had a phenomenal shot. When he scored 50 goals, 42 of them he scored with a snap shot. It was the best, quick release, just incredible. He would fan on [the puck] and it would still go in. Tony Esposito had nightmares about Mickey because he would shoot high. He would let one go up around the head just to let him know, 'Here it comes.' The times when he fanned on one, it would fool everybody. Even the goalies would see it coming and then watch helplessly as the puck trickled by, because it was like a changeup."

Redmond was a great friend to Dionne; amongst other lessons, he taught Marcel that there should be a balance to life. This meant enjoying oneself outside of the game. While Dionne loves to recall Mickey singing and strumming his guitar at house parties, he was equally influenced by Redmond's success in hockey. Unfortunately, Redmond developed serious back problems that ended his career. Again, Dionne was dismayed by the lack of compassion shown for his teammate. "Sometimes people forget to look at themselves. And those same people should learn to accept the people that surround them, as long as they're getting the job done on the ice. A lot of championship teams, and you might not hear about it, but they have dysfunctional people. But when it comes down to playing the game, *boom!* They get it done. In Detroit we suffered a little bit from that lack of acceptance. The way Mickey did things was different, so he became a target for ribbing. Sometimes I think it got to Mickey and he took it personally. But when he had his back surgery, that's when some players took it too far. They thought he was faking it. Well, c'mon, when a guy has surgery that leaves him with a zipper down his back he's not faking an injury. But Mickey's a survivor. He's still in Detroit, working as a broadcaster, doing his thing."

Behind the Red Wings bench at the beginning of 1973–74

(Dionne's third year with Detroit) was Ted Garvin, who would become another casualty of Detroit's revolving-door approach. After just 11 games, during which the team stumbled to a 2–8–1 record, Garvin was replaced by Alex Delvecchio. Delvecchio had entered the season as a player, but, at management's urging, decided that he might best help the team as coach. With the way things were going for the team, the situation could hardly get worse.

Bryan "Bugsy" Watson joined the Red Wings in a trade with St. Louis well after the midway point of that season. Expected to aid their troubled defence, Watson was put in the unfavourable position of having to make sense of the team's curious system. "Actually, it was quite funny," Watson starts. "I came to the Red Wings, it was my second time around with the team, and we were playing against the Montreal Canadiens. I had flown in, literally just in time for the game. Alex Delvecchio came up to me and said, 'Get dressed, have a look at our system from the bench, and try to pick up what you can. When we get back to Detroit we'll get you into the lineup.' Well, after the second period we're losing 8–2. So I walked into the dressing room and it was quiet as hell, and I said to the guys, 'If you didn't like the trade, why don't you just say so? You don't have to do this!' Everybody just howled.

"So we're playing the third period and Alex comes over to me. And remember that he had instructed me to look at the system. So he came down the bench and I said, 'Alex, I think I'm ready to play now. I've got your system down cold.' He said, 'Oh yeah, what's that?' I said, 'Just get it out of our end any f—in' way you can!' I don't know if he found that very funny."

The only consistency the Red Wings displayed was in missing the playoffs for the fourth consecutive year, and seventh time in the past eight. Nevertheless, while Dionne would certainly have preferred to be playing hockey through the spring of 1974, he and Carol did make good use of the time off.

"We eloped on April 5, 1974, in Detroit," Carol Dionne reports. "That season, I had moved in with Marcel; it was during

December of 1973. I told my mom that I had to find out if I would enjoy being home alone when he travelled with the team. I thought, 'What am I going to do, sit at home and knit?' My mother wasn't thrilled. I said, 'Don't worry, I've known him for five years!' So she agreed and we ended up having a different sort of wedding. Marcel said, 'We better elope now.' "

Being a very practical person, Marcel saw a window of opportunity and seized the day. One could also say that he has never been a fan of formal weddings and all that they entail.

"I think what happens with weddings is that there is always politics involved, too many people," Marcel says. "I still don't like weddings. I get a lot of invitations, but I seldom go. I prefer anniversary celebrations to weddings. For us, it was much easier to elope. We decided, no parents, no bullshit. Instead we invited the entire team. We got the marriage licence on Tuesday and got married on Friday—then we called our parents.

"I think in a perfect world it wouldn't work that way. I've had so many friends that live together for a long time, they get married, and the next day they get divorced. For me, the wedding was about commitment. I didn't want to have the big party and be tired and stressed out. Because I know her mom and I know my mom, and I know what they'd want—everything to be perfect. I came from a big family and I had been to enough weddings where everybody's crying and the mother is fighting with the bride over the flowers and whatever else. So we just got married and had one hell of a party. Later that summer we celebrated in St. Catharines with Carol's family and with mine in Drummondville—beautiful! In retrospect, I do wish our parents had been there for the wedding. If there was one thing we should have done, we should have at least invited them."

The 1974–75 season would be a pivotal one in Dionne's career. In his first three seasons he had been an offensive leader alongside

Mickey Redmond. Redmond had finished second to Dionne in points in two of the three years and edged him by three points in the other. With his commitment and his now-proven ability, Dionne was undeniably the Red Wings' best hope for a brighter future, and Alex Delvecchio, who was now doubling as coach and general manager, looked to him to embrace the status of team leader, a role that he accepted at the time but would come to see in a different light. "We were in Buffalo and Alex Delvecchio said to me, 'I would like you to be my captain.' It caught me off guard. And I don't think I should have been captain. It's a great honour, but junior hockey [Dionne had been captain in St. Catharines] and the NHL are two different things.

"I understand what they were trying to do with the captaincy, to show leadership and so on, but I think in some ways that's a lot of baloney. To be a leader you have to have the support, understanding, cooperation and respect of your teammates—they don't even have to like you, necessarily. To me, the captaincy was a nice gesture. But what does the captaincy really mean? Is it to be the player that addresses issues with the management? What is it?"

While Dionne clearly had the respect and support of his Detroit teammates from his leadership on the ice, his skills in dealing with the media had yet to be honed. The lack of experience in this regard ended up burning Marcel on more than one occasion. One of the more regrettable incidents followed a lacklustre outing in Montreal. Always under heightened scrutiny in his home province, where comparisons to the Canadiens' Guy Lafleur were still made, Dionne's inability to be anything but passionate and direct to a Montreal reporter cost him dearly after a frustrating loss.

"We'd gone into Montreal and the Canadiens had beaten us," says Nick Libett. "I remember it was the next day in the airport. Because Marce is from that area, obviously the press wanted to speak with him. Basically, after our loss, Marcel made a statement to a reporter and told him that there were only five guys on our team that were of NHL calibre—and he named the five players!

While it made me feel good to be one of the five players he named, it wasn't what you would call a unifying statement for the team."

As soon as the quote hit the papers, the shit hit the fan amongst Dionne's teammates. Bryan Watson was one individual who was quite comfortable in sending his own message in response.

"If you can imagine it, we were making a run for the playoffs, so Alex Delvecchio decided we should spend some time together as a team. So we were staying in this hotel in Detroit when we got the story. Well, I went and bought up all of these newspapers on the way to joining the guys for a team meal. I threw the whole stack of papers right on top of the table in front of Marcel, just to let him know what I thought.

"I don't know if I was on Marcel's list of players or not. The point I was trying to make was that if you're thinking about the team, if you exclude or include players on such a list, you're wrong either way. It was something he should have never done. There was no reason for it. They can say that it was outspoken on his part, but he was dead wrong. I challenged him on it because I was really pissed off, because there were a lot of guys that were really hurt. Who was he to judge? All he needed to do was to go out and play. But once I sent my message it was over with and we won our game the next night.

"I think what happened was that in Montreal Marcel got carried away and spoke his mind to some reporter, thinking it was off the record. Unfortunately, it got into the newspaper. You would never say that today and not expect it to be in the paper."

This predicament was a perfect example of why Dionne would continually be frustrated with, and would eventually shun, the leadership role and the related duties of team spokesperson. The passion and forthright manner that were fundamental to his personality were not qualities he could turn on and off for the media.

"I know that as captain you have to be able to handle the press. A lot of times when you see a captain who is not the best player, it is helpful to the player that is expected to produce. Because the player that is expected to produce is held accountable every game.

Later on, when I was asked to be captain in Los Angeles, I declined. I just didn't want it. I'll support the captain, give me an 'A' [making him an alternate captain], but I didn't think I was the guy."

Shots from the hip notwithstanding, Dionne's abundant desirable qualities, including the sincerity and dedication he had in spades, allowed his teammates to accept Marcel for the dynamic individual that he was, and take the good with the bad.

"That was Marcel," Libett assesses. "He didn't hold back on anything. I think he could have named a few more guys to his NHL-calibre list, Bryan Watson being one of them. But there were guys on those teams that Ned Harkness brought in that were definitely not NHL-calibre players. We had unloaded a bunch of people to other teams, quality players, and we didn't get much in return. And yeah, Marce was probably accurate in what he said. So Bryan took the newspapers, and Marce was sitting there and Bugsy threw them right in front him, turned his back and walked away. And now Marce and Bryan see each other all the time, they're best of friends."

While Dionne could have used a workshop in diplomacy for the team's sake, his game continued to prove that the Red Wings had a valuable commodity. In Montreal, the Canadiens management took notice of Dionne's progress while hoping to see similar results from Guy Lafleur.

"Marcel Dionne's first three years were a hell of a lot better than Guy Lafleur's first three years," recalls Dick Irvin, who was as familiar as anyone with the Canadiens in those days. "Guy Lafleur wasn't even considered for the rookie of the year award. Marcel scored 28 goals in his first season, 40 goals in his second year and 24 his third year. I mean, Marcel Dionne had quickly become a star. Guy Lafleur scored 29 goals in his first year, 28 goals his second, 21 goals his third year, and over his first three seasons looked like he might turn out to be a bust.

"Scotty Bowman told me this story where Sam Pollock had a meeting with Scotty and Claude Ruel. The question was, 'Do we keep Guy Lafleur or do we trade him? He only scored 21 goals in his third year, this guy's a bust.' And I can tell you from my experience broadcasting the games that Lafleur was a non-entity. The Canadiens won the Cup in 1973 and Lafleur didn't play a role in that at all. Now I don't know how serious this meeting was, but Sam Pollock asked the two coaches, 'Should we trade Lafleur? Let's get something for him if he's not going to work out.' However the conversation ended up, they decided they would take a chance on him for one more year.

"The next season for Lafleur was 1974–75, and I remember it like it was yesterday. They played the New York Islanders the first game of the season. Now, through the first three years of his career, Lafleur had worn a helmet. That night he skated out on the ice and he had no helmet. I remember doing the game with Danny Gallivan, and you were saying to yourself, 'Who *is* this guy?' He was *flying!* And he flew nonstop for the next six or seven years. But that season he played 70 games, scored 53 goals and 66 assists. He went from 56 points to 119 points in one year. And that was the start of Guy Lafleur. They didn't win the Stanley Cup that year, but they won it the next four.

"Later on that season, I had a conversation with Scotty on the way home from a game in Detroit. We used to come home on charter flights, and Scotty and I would regularly share a cab to our houses. He lived in Dorval, near the airport, and I lived in Pointe-Claire. It was a little out of my way, but that was okay. It gave me a chance to talk to Scotty one on one, and I never pressed him on anything, but you didn't have to press Scotty for anything, you know. Now, the Canadiens had just played this game in Detroit. My recollection is that the game ended up a 3–3 tie. Well, Dionne had scored all three of the goals for Detroit and he scored them on Dryden in three different ways, and he was absolutely outstanding. In the cab that night, Scotty said to me, 'Would you trade Ken Dryden for Marcel Dionne?' And I said, *'What?'* We had just come from Detroit, and Scotty said, 'That's what they want.' I guess they knew they weren't going to keep Dionne, so Scotty asked me that question because the Red Wings had made that offer."

One can only imagine the "what-if" scenario that would have played out had Marcel Dionne joined the Montreal Canadiens in 1975. While Lafleur exploded onto the scene that season with his 119 points, Marcel was equally magnificent with 121 points. The two players performing in their prime for the Canadiens would certainly have made for a remarkable display of firepower. However, it remains a moot point. Especially when one considers the wisdom Montreal showed in retaining the services of Ken Dryden. While Montreal fans would have loved the drama and the potent offence, would these have come at the cost of the record-breaking seasons and the four consecutive Stanley Cup titles in the late '70s? In any event, for the time being, Dionne was stuck in a thick Detroit fog.

As the 1974–75 season progressed, the Red Wings seemed as rudderless as ever. The situation gave Dionne little incentive to re-sign with the club at the end of this, the option year of his contract. While Marcel remained fully committed to the game, there existed more problems within the organization than one player could possibly change. Beyond the usual struggle in the standings, the latest blow to the team confirmed the decline in health of their leading goal scorer, Mickey Redmond.

"In those days you were more or less expected to play hurt. It just got to the point where I could not perform," remembers Redmond. "And performing for three hours was only part of it; after that, I couldn't move. Of course, when you've got a bad back, who knows what the exact problem is? A lot of people with bad backs would get looked upon as if, 'Yeah, but is he really hurt?' All I know is that when I ended up in the Mayo Clinic in Rochester, Minnesota, the doctor said, 'Why do they always send me you players when you're so buggered up that it's impossible to get you back to being 100 percent again? God, I wish they'd send me you guys when you're salvageable.' I ended up, at times, having to have my skates done up for me."

Redmond finished the 1974–75 season having played in only 29 of 80 games, and he struggled to play in 37 the following year before having to retire from the game. While Detroit had lost what had been a rare find in a 50-goal scorer, they managed to acquire Danny Grant, who hit the 50-goal mark in a career year playing alongside Dionne.

Nick Libett, who began the season on Dionne's line, recounted the good fortune he was forced to relinquish to Grant. "I often say that I was the main reason that Danny Grant scored 50 goals. I remember the first five games of that year. I played with Marcel and I had four goals in five games. Every year I would get my twenty-some goals, but they were expecting greater things from Danny. Well, after the five games he had none, or maybe one goal, with whomever he was playing with, so Alex made the switch. He put Danny on Marcel's line and moved me to play with whomever. I ended up with 23 goals and Danny got his 50 goals playing with Marcel.

"Marcel was so good offensively that you literally had what I call a bunch of lay-ups. I mean, you had to shoot the puck occasionally, but with the way that Marcel could handle the puck and see the ice, you'd just get in position and if you had any kind of knack around the net you'd score a bundle."

Despite Dionne's best season yet (47 goals, 74 assists), the Red Wings again missed the playoffs. The passion that burned inside of Dionne was sorrowfully lacking within the Detroit organization. Bryan Watson had been with the Montreal Canadiens and he could appreciate how Marcel's career might have been different had he joined the Canadiens.

"Marcel Dionne. There's a kid that, if he had been in Montreal, would have been ahead of Gordie [in terms of career points scored] and right on Gretzky's ass. Because Montreal demanded that you be a winner. Detroit didn't. Detroit was more of a country club. And when they were winning, it was a country club with great results. Believe me that it was a great team, and they always had great goaltenders. I'm going back to Sawchuk, Crozier and Glenn Hall. Then they had Ted Lindsay, and of course they always had Gordie Howe. So they had a tremendous base to start with. But Gordie was very casual. I mean, don't get me wrong, when he was on the ice he was intimidating and aggressive, and wanted to win as much or more than anyone in Montreal. But in the dressing room and off the ice, the team atmosphere was always casual. And this came from the top on down and had never changed because it was always the same people running the team.

"When I came from Montreal to Detroit—this was my first time with the Red Wings—I mean, Montreal was gung-ho. The players were always talking to each other in the dressing room, and at training camp the conversation was about whom we had to beat to get into first place and then to the Stanley Cup. It was all about the Stanley Cup from the day I arrived in Montreal as a nineteen-year-old.

"That's when we used to travel by train. You'd get on the train and head to the porter's room and the guys would have a beer after a game. You'd sit around, and there I was the rookie, sitting and listening to Geoffrion, Béliveau, Henri Richard, Fergie, Gump Worsley, all these guys tell stories *only* about the Montreal Canadiens. And they would talk about the great teams, the traditions, the championships, and the great players. Béliveau would tell stories about Dickie Moore and Doug Harvey. I can still recall sitting listening to Jean Béliveau and Geoffrion, who was so funny telling stories, and Jean-Guy Talbot. That's what tradition is all about. In Detroit you'd go into the dressing room, you'd be getting ready for a game, and guys are sitting there reading their mail. And of course I was so vocal. They must have thought I was nuts in Detroit, because I thought every team was like Montreal—and of course, it wasn't. And while Marcel probably accepted it in Detroit, deep down it didn't sit well with him."

In 1974–75, Dionne was forced to address his future with an organization that had yet to earn his loyalty. In some ways he was happy in Detroit; it was, and remains, a great hockey town. Nevertheless, not all of the experiences Dionne had with the club left him longing to remain a Red Wing. The steady flow of players on and off their roster, the incompetence of management, the implications of the despicable treatment of Gordie Howe, and Dionne's own problems adjusting to his leadership role all forced him to consider his options.

Throughout the physical setbacks Mickey Redmond had faced that year he remained close to Dionne. When all of these issues were running through Marcel's mind it was Redmond who served as his sounding board. "Mickey and I shared a lot of information, which in those days was frowned upon. He's actually the main reason why I left Detroit. The Red Wings had offered me a new contract—$175,000 a year for five years. I was sitting in the back of the bus with Mickey, and he told me that he was making somewhere around $200,000 a year. And I even liked the deal they offered me. I said, 'Hey, I'm happy.' Mickey said, 'You know, there's more money than that. I'm telling you right now.' That's when the WHA was around. I said, 'What do you mean?' He said, 'Marcel, I'm not kidding you, you've got to ask for more money.'

"Eagleson was my agent at the time, and I talked to him, and the Red Wings gave him permission to look around. When he started to see the interest that was out there, I soon realized that Mickey was right. But at that time I was sorting out another problem with the Detroit organization. You see, some of the players were incorporated, as in Marcel Dionne Enterprises. So, you were allowed to take your salary from the team as a deduction to your company. It was allowed up to a point where the IRS decided one day that you were no longer able to do that. So it ended up that there was a $45,000 discrepancy with the IRS. I was negotiating my new contract with the Red Wings and I had that expense in mind. Who was going to pay that money: the Red Wings or Marcel Dionne? If I had to cover it, then I had to make $80,000 or $90,000 more to pay it back. That became a big issue while I had the offer of $175,000. So, Eagleson talked with them, and the Red Wings came back and said, 'If he signs with us, we'll pay the $45,000; if he doesn't, *he* owes the IRS.' And that's when they told Eagleson to go ahead and shop me around.

"Instead of trying to resolve the issue with Detroit, Eagleson started to look around. Well, Montreal offered $200,000; St. Louis offered money, but they were afraid that they would have to give up Garry Unger as compensation; and then Los Angeles came out of nowhere with an offer of $300,000. That became a real dilemma, because I really didn't want to leave Detroit. Suddenly I was all confused."

Mickey Redmond continues: "Marcel was trying to sign a new contract, and my understanding was that they were playing games with him at the time. They told him, 'Go ahead and shop your wares if you think you're worth more.' I didn't encourage him; I said, 'As far as I'm concerned, Marcel, as a friend, I feel like I have to tell you that you probably should go ahead and shop your wares.' As much as I hated to lose him, as a friend, I felt I had to tell him that. I was obligated to do that.

"If you look back in time, Marcel may be considered one of the first people to force a move. He ended up signing a great contract with Jack Kent Cooke in Los Angeles. The Detroit Red Wings were forced to make a deal to accommodate that, almost like today's situation with a restricted free agent. But this was done way before those rules were ever written. My understanding was that they said to him, 'If you think you're more valuable, then go ahead and shop your wares elsewhere.' I would say that it was a rather foolish move by the organization. Marcel did, and the rest is history."

When Dionne's contract expired at the conclusion of his fourth season, he was a free agent. However, Detroit's exclusive rights to his services extended only as far as the National Hockey League. One option that remained open to him, and which had been exercised by dozens of high-profile NHLers, was to jump leagues and sign with a team in the World Hockey Association. To establish itself as a credible alternative, the WHA needed to lure marquee players from the NHL. The owners of WHA franchises had already succeeded offering healthy contracts to the likes of Bobby Hull, Gordie Howe and Frank Mahovlich. Even those NHL players who weren't intent on jumping leagues benefited from the

WHA's presence; the presence of a rival league gave the stars unprecedented leverage in contract negotiations. Dionne's ace in the hole was an offer from the Edmonton Oilers. "Edmonton offered me $250,000 Canadian a year for five years. That offer came from Bill Hunter, who said, 'That's the richest contract ever. Nobody is making that kind of money.' I never told him that I had an offer for $300,000 U.S. from Los Angeles."

Though the Edmonton offer wasn't the most lucrative, it held a strategic value all its own. Marcel wasn't truly a free agent; any team Dionne agreed to terms with would have to pay compensation, in the form of players, to Detroit. The Wings would be hard-pressed to replace a talent like Dionne, and therefore might not be fully motivated to make a deal that suited Marcel. The Oilers opportunity meant the Wings no longer had complete control over his future; if Marcel jumped, they'd be left empty-handed.

With several offers on the table, Dionne was about to make the most critical decision of his career. "I was still thinking that I would like to play in Detroit. Alex Delvecchio was the coach and general manager, and I wanted to play for Alex. So I went back to Detroit with Eagleson and he said, 'You know what? I think you need a fresh start. We're going to call the Red Wings right now and tell them you're not coming back.'"

Chapter Seven

SHORTLY AFTER the conclusion of the 1974–75 season, Dionne joined Mickey Redmond and a couple of his buddies for a brief vacation of golf and sunshine in Miami. As he enjoyed himself down south he was still getting his head around his mixed emotions about staying in Detroit. From the moment he was drafted by the Red Wings, Dionne had represented the team's future. Unfortunately, in each of the four seasons he played in Detroit, the team had been unable to make the playoffs. With no indication that this trend would change, he saw Los Angeles as an opportunity to start over.

In the midst of their vacation, in a last-ditch attempt to convince him to remain with the Red Wings, Detroit owner Bruce Norris invited Dionne and company to his yacht club. The itinerary included lunch and an afternoon of fishing aboard his yacht. Inevitably, meeting with Norris only served to confirm to Marcel that the plight of the Red Wings wasn't about to change in the foreseeable future, nor was it a cross he wished to bear any longer. "Bruce Norris had a drinking problem. It was very well known. So I'm twenty-one years old, I see this man come into the room half in the bag, and I say to myself, 'Wow, *this* is an NHL owner?' I mean, you'd go upstairs and he would have ladies of the night with him most of the time. I think the guys prior to me, like Alex and Gordie, they understood Bruce Norris. But for me, Bruce would come in—'Hi, how's it going?'—and he was half in the bag. He knew who all of the players were, but I never got the feeling that he cared enough. And I felt that way because he was the guy that hired Ned Harkness and his group—who never did anything to me personally, but it showed there was no strength in the ownership."

Upon arriving at the yacht club with Redmond and party in tow, Dionne was mildly apprehensive about being in such raucous company in what appeared to be a very prestigious establishment. Redmond's hazy recollections of the meeting indicate that it was a valid concern. "I'm not even sure why we were there. It probably would have been over Marcel's contract, I would think. It was a fiasco—that much I do remember. I know we had a couple of buddies with us, and at one point Marce said to me, 'Mickey, you're going to get me thrown out of here!'" Redmond laughs, "The guys were acting up. Without giving too much detail, let's just say the guys were having a few beers."

Eventually, over the course of the afternoon, Norris had the opportunity to take Dionne aside and say his piece. While Dionne had initially expressed his intention to re-sign with the club, he got the feeling that Norris was going through the motions in his final sales pitch. "He wanted to talk to me alone. He said, 'We want you and it's important for you to stay with the organization.' But that wasn't good enough for me—so we went fishing. And that was the last time I spoke to Bruce Norris."

In the end, the only significant draw for Dionne to remain in Detroit was Alex Delvecchio. Having had the fortune to play with a Hall of Famer whom he held in the highest regard meant a great deal to him. That he was not able to succeed for Delvecchio in a manner he would have liked was the one disappointment in his decision to leave Detroit. "I still see Alex. To this day I tell him how sorry I am. He was a great coach and a great person to me. I love that guy. When I left, he ripped me apart: I was a loser, a selfish player. Hey, I understood his position, but I never took the ripping too seriously. When I see him today, it's great. He still calls me Beaver. 'Hey, Beav, how's it going?' And I love it.

"When you talk about legends, to me this guy is a legend. I'll tell you a story about Alex and what I thought of him. Here was a guy that rarely missed a game due to injury. And I didn't miss many games myself before I broke my collarbone in junior. So I'm in Detroit, and the trainer was Lefty Wilson. This one time I went to see Lefty, and I got up on the first aid table. Well, getting treatment and a rubdown felt pretty good. Alex came into the room, and now I had to answer to the master. He said, 'What's wrong with you?' I said, 'Well, uhh, I'm aching somewhere.' He said, 'You know what? If you lay down there too long, you're going to start liking it. That's not going to be good for you.' And after that I never went back. I may have gone when I absolutely had to, but I've seen guys that get to like first aid rooms and become hypochondriacs. It's like they become addicted to the trainer's room. So early on I learned from Alex that the more you stay away from the trainer's room, the better you'll become at playing through the minor things. That was a lesson from one of the great ones."

The time spent in Detroit had in fact taught Dionne many lessons. Although he might have preferred to have had more guidance through his green days, experience itself proved to be an effective teacher. "I still wonder why Alex or Gary Bergman didn't take me aside and say, 'Here's what's going on.' We would talk about the game, but I never had anyone explain what was going on in the big picture. Even if I had, it probably wouldn't have mattered. I was very stubborn and was probably spoiled with having things go my way. In Detroit, all of a sudden things weren't going my way.

"There were things I did in certain situations that I wish I had been more mature about. Because we were losing all the time, I would want to take charge. If you're playing well and some other guys aren't, you're not supposed to go and tell them they're playing like shit or say, 'You guys need to get off your asses.' I would say things like that, and understandably it wouldn't go over well. But in my rookie year I would challenge anybody—absolutely," Dionne laughs, "and Alex would say, 'Ahh, Kid, shut up.' What I needed was some refinement off the ice."

With each passing season in Detroit, Marcel had improved on and off the ice. However, it would be some time yet before Dionne would be the player he wanted to be. Appropriately, of all the memories he would take from Detroit, the most important came from his rookie season. It was the feeling he got when he played against the men he aspired to be like. "The things I did individually were not important to me. What had me in awe was watching my idols. The one-two combination of Bobby Orr and Phil Esposito for the Boston Bruins, or when I was on the ice when Bobby Hull scored his fiftieth goal in Chicago that year. I mean, when you score fifty goals in the NHL today, or even in my day, it means nothing. When I saw Bobby Hull score his fiftieth, the [crowd at] Chicago Stadium went nuts. And he just smoked it. That's what hockey's all about. Playing against Stan Mikita, playing against Frank Mahovlich with the Montreal Canadiens, Davey Keon, Bob Pulford—Henri Richard, for Chrissakes. Can you imagine? To me, my first year, every game I was in awe. I have so much respect for all of those guys. It's because of them I'm where I am today."

The Los Angeles Kings had joined the NHL as one of six new teams in the 1967 league expansion. Team owner Jack Kent Cooke hoped to draw fans to the games by having such recognizable names on the team's roster as Terry Sawchuk, Dick Duff, Bob Pulford, Ralph Backstrom and Harry Howell. Given that proven talent tended to be rather long in the tooth, the Kings' strategy aimed for short-term gain. It could also be a costly one, as was the case when they acquired Eddie Shack from Boston and gave up two first-round draft picks in return. By 1975, what the L.A. Kings desperately needed were some good young players. If Marcel Dionne was looking forward to a fresh start with a clean slate, Los Angeles was a suitable destination.

The makeup of the team was that of a group of gritty players who relied heavily on their All-Star goaltender, Rogie Vachon. Having won three Stanley Cups with the Montreal Canadiens in his first five years in the league, Vachon was a solid base that any team could build upon. While he could have remained in Montreal after the arrival of Ken Dryden, he wasn't interested in playing second fiddle, nor did he want to wait for his hand to be played out at a later date.

"I was playing for Montreal, and at the end of the 1970–71 season Ken Dryden got out of college and they gave him six games to play at the end of the schedule—and he did very well. They decided to start him in the playoffs. Well, we won the Stanley Cup that year, and Ken wound up being the most valuable player in the playoffs and all that good stuff. I was still young in those days and I figured, 'I don't want to be the number two goalie,' so I went to Sam Pollock and I asked to be traded. I told him, 'I don't care where I go, it doesn't matter, I just want to play,' and I ended up in L.A."

If it was ice time he wanted, it was ice time he got. Parachuted onto a team of questionable ability, Vachon immediately had his work cut out for him. Making the job that much more challenging was the reality that, in those early days of expansion, there were—aside from the Seals in Oakland—no teams playing anywhere near L.A. Needless to say, the toll the travel exacted from the team didn't make Vachon's considerable load any lighter.

"It was certainly a culture shock. When you go from a Stanley Cup winner to a team that was very weak, you could say it wasn't pretty. The New York Rangers had a great team, Montreal had a great team, the Boston Bruins were a powerhouse, and we had to travel in those days and play seven or eight road games in a row. And that was all done on commercial flights, which made it even more difficult. All of a sudden you'd wind up at the end of one of these runs, everybody is tired, and you've got to go into Madison Square Garden and play the seventh or eighth game of a road trip. Some nights I would keep the other team to six or seven goals and be quite pleased with it."

With the addition of Vachon for the 1971–72 season and a coaching change the following year that put Bob Pulford at the helm, the Kings began to move in a positive direction. In '74–75 the Kings tallied a surprising 105 points in the standings, a franchise record that stands to this day. In recognition of that considerable accomplishment, Pulford won the Jack Adams Award as coach of the year. Certain players were key to the team's success, among the most important of whom was their rugged leader, Dan Maloney. When it became evident that the Kings were pursuing the services of Marcel Dionne, Pulford took pains to ensure the nucleus of the team remained intact.

"I remember Bob Pulford telling me that he drove to Mr. Cooke's home in Bel Air with a list of players and he said, 'I do not want these players traded for Marcel Dionne,'" recalls Bob Miller, the longtime broadcaster for the Kings. "And Mr. Cooke said, 'Oh, I wouldn't trade these players for Marcel Dionne.' Then Bob said to me, 'As I drove back home I thought, Wait a minute. Cooke said, "I wouldn't trade *all* of these players."' Bob told me that he turned right around, went back and said, 'Mr. Cooke, I don't want you to trade any *one* of these players for Marcel Dionne.' And Dan Maloney was on that list. Well, Cooke went ahead and traded Maloney. So that got Pully a little upset."

The trade that was finalized with the Detroit Red Wings on June 23, 1975, sent Marcel Dionne and Bart Crashley to L.A. in exchange for Dan Maloney, Terry Harper and a second-round pick in the next year's amateur draft. Mike Murphy, a good friend and longtime teammate of Dionne in L.A., understood Pulford's frustration, as well as the awkward spot that was created for Dionne.

"It was a tough situation to come into because the team had really overachieved the year before Marcel arrived. And it was a team that was fairly tight knit," Murphy says. "Maloney was one of our leaders, Terry Harper was another one of our leaders, and they were both dealt to Detroit for Marcel. At the time, our best player was our goalie, Rogie Vachon. The team was structured in such a way that we weren't very good offensively. Pulford knew that and designed a system of play where Vachon could make the big saves and we'd clear the rebounds. So we won all of our games 3–2, 2–1, 1–0, and we had a very successful year. But that wasn't the type of entertaining hockey that Cooke wanted. And it wasn't the type of hockey that was going to endure for a long period of time, especially with the makeup of our team."

While Detroit was fortunate to do as well as it did with the trade, Los Angeles undoubtedly got the better of the deal. However, in neglecting to consult Bob Pulford *or* the Kings' general manager, Jake Milford, Cooke caused irreparable damage to the relationship between himself and his management team.

"Pully was a very loyal coach. In other words, he was a players' coach," Vachon says. "He would tell the guys, 'Listen, if you play my system the way I tell you to, you're going to stay here—I won't trade you. We're all going to do this together.' So we were like a big family. Then Jack Kent Cooke decided to trade for Marcel, and we gave up Terry Harper and Dan Maloney. Well, Dan Maloney was our enforcer, our big guy, so initially a lot of teammates were upset. And Pulford was upset because it went against his philosophy. These guys played well for us and were traded away. I guess Pully felt he lost face with the players a little bit, and he ended up quitting later on."

Before Dionne got to meet his new teammates, he went to Los Angeles for a press conference that would introduce him as the latest addition to the Kings. To ensure that his promising young star made the right first impression, Jack Kent Cooke met with him prior to addressing the media. "When I walked into the meeting, Jack Kent Cooke said, 'Let's sit down here.' And he was very articulate when he spoke. He said, 'Young man, do you know how much of your brain you actually use?' I thought to myself, 'Holy shit, he's really got me on this one.' I said, 'You know what? It's funny you ask, because a few weeks ago I read an article that said we only use 5 percent of our brain.' I may have said another number, but I know it was very low because I didn't want to say anything too high. And he said, 'Young man, that is why you are sitting there and I am sitting here.' And it was true. This guy was a brain. Here's a man that almost went broke and ended up with an empire. He was in telecommunications, he owned the Los Angeles Lakers, the Washington Redskins, and he built the Los Angeles Forum.

"So at this meeting he said, 'I'm going to ask you a few questions and I want you to pretend that I am the press.' And he went through a series of questions with me. 'What do you think of this trade?' 'What do you think of Los Angeles?' I was quite impressed by that, because I had never spent that much time with an owner—and the press conference went very well. So we agreed upon a contract, which by the way was a handshake, and Eagleson and I returned home. I never actually signed a contract until I got a letter from Clarence Campbell that said that I had to sign one or I couldn't play. I think it was two or three months after our meeting with Cooke. I was hoping to defer my pay to January 1, 1976, for tax purposes."

Later that summer, Dionne's good feelings about L.A. were reinforced when he met his new teammate Mike Murphy at a golf tournament. While he knew that the trading of Maloney wasn't a popular move amongst the Kings, he was pleased to hear Murphy be direct and honest about Cooke's decision. Murphy plainly acknowledged the loss and countered, ". . . but we got Marcel Dionne in return."

More good news for the Dionne family came on August 12, 1975, when Carol and Marcel's first-born arrived, a baby girl they named Lisa. With a newborn to care for, Carol remained with her family in St. Catharines while Marcel went off to training camp with the Kings, after which he would find a home for the family in L.A.

Upon joining his new team, Marcel discovered that fitting in wasn't going to be as smooth as he had first thought. It was clear that several players' loyalty to the traded personnel was still lingering in the dressing room.

Bob Miller talks about getting to know Dionne: "I first met Marcel in Victoria, British Columbia, where we had training camp. He and I kind of hit it off; however, I don't know how well he was received by the players. It seemed to me that Marcel was always kind of going around on his own, so I went along with him a few times, shopping and stuff like that. I got the impression—

now, it may be the wrong impression because I'm not in the locker room hanging around all of the time—but I got the impression that there wasn't an open-arms reception for Marcel."

If there was one person Marcel did expect to be cool towards him, it was his new coach. Pulford had gone as far as to let it be known publicly that he disapproved of the trade. Not surprisingly, when Dionne—who was now the highest-paid player in the history of the game—arrived, Pulford gave him the cold shoulder. "Bob Pulford didn't say much when I first went there," Dionne says. "Not too many guys were talking to me. Rogie did, and Bob Nevin did. Guys talked, but they didn't say much. They just didn't know me yet. I suppose I had this stigma, that I must have been a bad guy, someone who was selfish. Perhaps that's what they had heard for the last four years."

Jack Kent Cooke's dealing had effectively driven a wedge between Dionne and his coach. As a result of this fumbled beginning, once the season got under way, Marcel didn't have the spectacular jump from the gates that Cooke expected for his dollar. While Gilbert Perreault was headed for a career year and Guy Lafleur would win the NHL scoring title in 1975–76, a period of adjustment was needed before Marcel was effectively worked into the Kings' game plan. In response to this delayed ignition, the hands-on owner called him in for a meeting. Typically, he did so in a manner that would further compromise Dionne's standing with the coaching staff and his teammates. Recognizing Cooke's disregard for the chain of command, Dionne insisted on setting things straight.

"I came into practice one day and there was a note written on the chalkboard. It said, 'Marcel, go see Mr. Cooke.' On the frickin' chalkboard. So all the guys were like, 'What's the owner want to talk with you for? Haven't you got a coach, a general manager to talk to?' Talking shop with the owner was a no-no. So that was a stupid move. Whatever Cooke had to say to me, all he had to do was have Bob Pulford come and talk to me. But Jack Kent Cooke would do things like that. That was his way.

"So now I've got to go upstairs and some of the guys are snickering. Like Butch Goring, who was always talking out of the side of his mouth—'Hey, fat cat, what's going on here?' I go up to his office and I have no clue what he wants, and the secretary tells me, 'Mr. Cooke will be with you shortly.' I get into his office—and it always seemed that his seat was very high up and when you would sit down you'd be sinking in the chair. So I'm looking up at him, and he says, 'Young man, I'd like to talk to you. I'm paying you all of this money and I look at Gilbert Perreault and these other players, and they are all doing very well and you're not doing so well. What's going on?' When he said that, I thought to myself, 'Oh, great, I'm a dead man.' I knew where this was headed, and I knew better than to go there. I had never—and wouldn't consider telling a coach to play me with someone specific, or tell a general manager to do this or that, like 'Trade this guy,' which I know has happened. I never did that.

"Now, I understood that Mr. Cooke was trying to get something out of me. So I said, 'I'll talk to you, but I think it's unfair to do it this way. I might say something that you will misinterpret. To prevent that, I would rather have Bob Pulford here and we'll discuss it.' And he said, 'Would you like to have Jake [Milford] here, too?' I said, 'That would be fine.'

"So he called them in, and I have never been so embarrassed in my life. There I was, just petrified as the player, and in walk my coach and general manager and I can see that they don't even want to talk to this guy. At the time, I didn't know what Cooke was like or what these people had been through. And Bob Pulford and Jake Milford were two good guys. We got talking, and I said, 'Mr. Cooke, Bob's been good to me as a coach, and I don't want to tell him what to do. But there are certain ways I think I could be of help to the team. For instance, at the start of a game, if I'm given the go-ahead, sometimes I score the first goal to give us the edge right away. And there are things that I have to work on with Bob as well.'

"So we had the meeting, and I left and they continued talking.

But I waited a half an hour for Bob. When he returned to his office, I walked in and said, 'Bob, I'm really sorry about all of this. It's a fresh start for me here. I just want to make sure that you're okay with everything I said. In Detroit, I never dealt with management or went behind anyone's back. It was always up front with the players. And I've never asked to play on a line with this guy or that guy.' And he said to me, 'Marcel, I had respect for you before you came here, but today I have a great deal more respect for you. So I thank you for the meeting today.' That was huge in getting Bob and I on the right track."

Apart from the holes Dionne had to climb out of with his coach and teammates over the trade, he also had to overcome the latest unflattering depiction of him in the newspapers. Marrying his body type to his handsome salary, the press slammed him at the first chance they got. "Our first game was in Montreal, then we went on to play the Islanders and Rangers. But that first game, we just got killed and the press hit me with the $300,000 angle. They said I was rich and overweight, just condemning me. Yet our sport had been so far behind all of the other major league sports as far as wealth for the athletes. And then several players said in the papers that I received too much money, or that I didn't deserve that kind of money. Instead, why didn't they say, 'He's the guy that opened the door for everyone? Now we all have a chance to make decent money.'"

Being under the microscope, now more so than ever, Dionne had to perform at the top of his game every night just to silence his critics. The residual benefit of this attention was that when he did his job game in and game out, the rest of the Kings had to elevate their play or be left holding the bag. On this score, Dionne remembered the first show of support that came from Pulford on their first road trip. "Following the game in Montreal, we played the Islanders and got murdered again. Then we went to play against the Rangers and we won, but just barely. After the first period of that game, Bob Pulford came into the room and he was really pissed off. He said, 'I want to tell you guys something—and

Marcel, this has nothing to do with you. A lot of you guys aren't pulling your weight here.' From that point on, I started to blend in with the team."

After the endorsement from his coach, it wasn't long before Dionne won the favour of his teammates. Now that the connection had been made in Los Angeles on the team front, Dionne would have to address his personal life and settle his family on the west coast. While in Montreal for their first game, he was able to have a few short hours with Carol and baby Lisa, whom he had not seen in over three weeks. Although Carol had gone long stretches without her husband before, her first taste of motherhood without the presence of a supporting spouse was a true test for their future.

"Carol was somewhat depressed when Lisa was born, which I believe is normal," says Marcel. "She was with my family in Quebec, and she had her mother around, but I don't think she was prepared for all the moves we were making. A lot of times we talk about the lives of the players and what men do, but part of that is family. I think that everybody wants to spend time with their family, because family is the most important thing. And I don't want to sound harsh, but for me hockey was also number one. Hockey has given me everything, and that trickles down. My wife learned at a very young age that she would run into problems that I wouldn't always be around to help her with. And that's the trade-off.

"Sometimes we forget what it's like to be married to an athlete. I'm gone for two and three weeks, having a good time with the boys, and she is looking after the home. I think the experience of having Lisa [combined with] me going off to L.A. made her tougher. I remember when I met her in Montreal; I thought it was strange because it was the first time I had ever seen my wife cry. And my wife never cries; she's a strong lady. I think at that time she was scared of the unknown—having to move to Los Angeles and not knowing what would happen there."

Carol replies: "I was anxious because I hadn't seen Marcel, I just had Lisa and I wanted to hear what he had to say about L.A. Was he happy? Did the coach like him? And I asked him, 'How are the people there?' He kept telling me they were great. Well, when I moved to Los Angeles, I found out for myself."

In many ways, the life of a hockey spouse is quite similar to that of the hockey player. Days, and sometimes weeks, are spent apart during each month of the hockey season. Along with the separation, both partners feel the demands and stresses of the high-profile career; at the same time, unexpected changes require flexibility and resiliency from both parties. Strangely enough, in Carol's case, the biases against her "overpaid" husband seemed to have greater effect on her day-to-day life than it did Marcel's.

"When I first got to know the wives in L.A., they were very cold towards me. Marcel was making more money than the average player there, and when the wives would get together, they would ask, 'How much does your husband make?' Well, I couldn't reveal how much Marcel was making because I knew it was more than everybody else. I would tell them that I hadn't seen the contract and I didn't know. But I knew how much it was, and I could feel the resentment caused by it. The other part of the problem was that the wives in Los Angeles were very close to the wives of the players who were traded. They were the leaders in their group, but I wasn't a leader or a follower. I preferred to do my own thing outside of hockey. So when I went to the games, and went to the wives' room, nobody would talk to me. I remember being at a team Christmas party and one of the girls told me to f— off! It was horrible."

Ironically, where Dionne's contract inspired jealousy amongst his colleagues, there should have been gratitude. Because Marcel had the sense to seek out the best situation for himself and his family, and the guts to absorb the backlash over the deal he was offered, players' salaries increased throughout the league in the years that immediately followed.

While Marcel Dionne's acumen warrants recognition, he would suggest it is Bobby Hull who truly deserves the lion's share of the credit. When Hull signed his contract with the Winnipeg Jets of the WHA in 1972, he instantly gave credibility to the new league, which in turn destroyed the monopoly held by the NHL owners. Other players followed Hull's lead, which in turn forced NHL owners to pay their players fair market value or risk losing them.

Shortly after the beginning of the season, the Dionnes settled in Los Angeles. Both Marcel and Carol were happy in their new home. Although Carol felt the bitterness over the disparity in income for several years, Marcel brushed it off for what it was worth. "It was like that everywhere in those days. I didn't pay attention to it. It was really immature, but that goes on all the time. It died down when everybody started to make good money."

The compensation that Dionne received was indeed being earned with his own sweat and blood. Consequently, the Los Angeles Kings added a new dimension to their game, a factor that came as a great relief to their overworked netminder, Rogie Vachon. "When Marcel joined us, he started popping the goals and all of a sudden we were coming back from behind when we were down by one or two. Prior to Marcel's arrival, that was very difficult. We had to get the lead and just sit on it. That's how we were successful. If we had a 1–0 lead, especially on the road, we'd send one guy in and leave four guys on the red line. With Marcel in our lineup—he gave us much more depth, more offence, especially on the power play."

In joining the Los Angeles Kings and finding a way to fit in despite trying circumstances, Dionne had taken massive steps towards maturing as a hockey player and a team leader. Throughout that first season he would face many challenges, from the demands of management to the expectations of his teammates. Oddly enough, of all the battles he won that year, his greatest victory came in a game the Kings lost to Detroit.

To simply state that Marcel Dionne had left the Red Wings and their fans for greener pastures would be a gross understatement. In the eyes of the Detroit hockey community, he had betrayed the organization and denied it its franchise player. When Dionne returned for the first time as a Los Angeles King, he was in for a rude welcome.

"I would have loved to leave Detroit on better terms, because when I went back it was chaos, a riot. They had big signs everywhere saying stuff like 'Pee on Dionne' and 'Dionne's a Traitor.' It was a chance for them to show that I was the cause of all their problems. I was so nervous I didn't sleep the night before. I knew it was going to be a war, and I warned the team, but nobody was prepared for what happened. It was, 'Let's get this guy.' The game was sold out and you just knew it; even during the warmup, every time I touched the puck, they booed—real loud. Then, right from the first shift, [the Wings] were running the shit out of me—I mean big time."

Dionne's old teammate Bryan Watson recalled how Marcel responded to the outpouring of abuse. "Marcel showed me a tremendous amount of courage when he came back into Detroit. Dennis Polonich just went after him unmercifully, and Marcel wouldn't back down. He just played his game and played extremely well. I mean, Polonich ran him, slashed him, hooked him and cut him, and he never backed down. That showed me a side of Marcel that I had never seen before. I knew the guy had grit and balls just by the way he played the game. But up until that point, I had never realized that when he was really pushed, he could rise to the occasion like that. I gained a tremendous amount of respect for him in that game alone. It was really tough."

Viewing the game in its entirety would reveal that it wasn't merely a one-man assault against Dionne. Through sixty minutes of punishing hockey, the entire Red Wings team laid down the gauntlet. Indeed, it was a day of reckoning for Dionne on many levels. "There were fights everywhere. I remember being on the ice when everyone had paired off—and for some reason I ended up with Dan Maloney. We had met back in St. Catharines—I was playing junior there while Chicago was running their training camp, which he was at. Now all of a sudden I'm in the middle of a brawl and we've paired off. Well, I knew he had a lot on his mind, and I knew he loved L.A. I mean, he *loved* L.A. So I'm thinking to myself, 'Oh shit, here it comes.' But I was ready. If he suckers me, I'm ready to go. I recall that I said something to the effect of, 'I'm sorry about this whole thing.' And that was a really emotional moment. He could have killed me, and the fans were screaming and wanted him to, but Dan never swung."

Perhaps fittingly, the player that got the best piece of Dionne was his old linemate, Nick Libett. "Of all the guys to get me it had to be Nick Libett, my old left winger. And I don't mind being hit, because I'm going to hit you right back. But Nick really nailed me with a check. I thought he broke my arm. It was hyper-extended and it went this way and that way. I finished the game, but I was in pain."

Like the majority of the aggression that was being channelled towards him, Libett's was enhanced by Marcel's decision to leave the Red Wings. According to Libett, now that he was the opposition, Dionne got the treatment he deserved: "I do recall the game, and I will also say that I like Marcel. But in those days Marcel was no longer a Red Wing—he was a Los Angeles King and we were on the ice to win the hockey game. There might have been more intensity from our end, but it was by no means with intent to hurt him. But the hit I had on him, if I can recall, was in his own end, just inside the blue line. I caught him with a check, and it was clean because there was no penalty on the play."

After learning that Marcel thought the bodycheck had broken his arm, Libett added, "Yeah, I hit him quite hard, that I remember." Laughs Nick, "And if you see him, tell him that twenty-five years later, I'm still not sorry!"

To the astonishment of the Kings, the scene that followed the Detroit homecoming was absolute bedlam, not unlike the turmoil during the junior playoff series against the Quebec Remparts a few years before. Despite the fact that the Red Wings had won the hard-fought game, the crowd's appetite for revenge had not been sated. Outside the Olympia, an incensed horde threatened Dionne and surrounded the Kings' bus. While his teammates jokingly probed Marcel as to what he had done to those people, security guards made arrangements to have the bus pull up flush against the arena door to allow for a safe departure.

In the dressing room, Dionne was nursing his battered arm as he awaited the inevitable onslaught of questions from the press. Again, it would be Bob Pulford who backed him when the chips were down. "I had taken off my equipment and Bob Pulford came right over to me—and I'll never forget this. He put one foot up on the bench and said, 'I'm going to be with you, standing right beside you to make sure that you're not misquoted.' And he said, 'Remember one thing: these guys fought hard for you tonight.' I went through my interview and answered everyone. But more importantly, I had the utmost respect for Bob Pulford and what he did.

"After the game, I was hoping to visit with some of my friends from Detroit. Well, with everything that had gone on, my mind wasn't where it should have been. I said to Bob, 'I would like to go out with some friends, if that would be all right.' And that's when I learned what Pully meant by team, and why he didn't want to lose Dan Maloney. Bob said, 'Why don't you come back to the hotel on the bus with the team? They played hard for you tonight. Be on the bus; when we get to the hotel you can meet up with your friends.' After that, I said to myself that I would never let that man down."

Hardship and adversity frequently bring people together. For the Dionne-era Kings, from that point on, playing in Detroit would have that effect to a profound degree. "We actually developed a great deal of cohesion that night," Mike Murphy attests. "We didn't win the game, but we stuck to it and battled every inch of the way. And they really went out to get Marcel. He was beaten up over the course of the game with slashes, high hits, cross-checks. We endured that game, after which I don't think we lost to the Red Wings in Detroit for another fifteen or sixteen games straight. We went on a real spree. Every time we played them it was a big game."

Being the competitor that he was, Dionne came away from the Detroit episode with an understanding that there was only one way to put an end to the fans' animosity. That solution had become a recurring theme in his life. "After we lost that game, when I came back to Detroit, I thought, 'Never again will I go through that.' I ended up playing some of my greatest hockey against the Detroit Red Wings in Detroit—two-, three-, four-goal nights. The only way I was going to shut them up was to just be outstanding. I can remember a game in Detroit that I scored four goals in; it was against Rogie Vachon, after he left L.A., and by the end of the game they were cheering me. For years after that, when I'd come back from L.A. they'd cheer."

Chapter Eight

B Y THE END of Dionne's first year in Los Angeles he had assimilated nicely into the Kings organization. While the 1975–76 season started out with an initial period of adjustment, Marcel finished with respectable numbers (40 goals and 54 assists). A further validation of his worth came that summer when Dionne once again received an invitation to represent his country on the ice.

For Marcel Dionne, Team Canada '76 would finally afford him the opportunity he missed in 1972, to compete amongst the greatest players in the game. While nothing could match the drama of the original edition of Team Canada, Dionne is certain that the calibre of the team was on a par. "The 1972 Canada–Russia series was probably the greatest series of all time, but for me the biggest team to be a part of was Team Canada '76. If you look at the lineup, most of the guys went on to the Hall of Fame—it's incredible."

Having learned from the gaffes of the 1972 program, the organizers of the new Canada Cup saw to it that things ran considerably more smoothly for the Canadian side. Rather than a series consisting of an even number of games—which created the potential for a tie—a tournament format was designed, one which would include the six major hockey nations, Canada, the U.S.S.R., the United States, Czechoslovakia, Sweden and Finland. Canada also took a simplified approach towards building its roster. As Gilbert Perreault recalls, "It was different in '76 because they kept it down to 25 or so players [there were 27 players, excluding goalies, which was significantly less than the bloated '72 roster that had 32 skaters]. Also, in 1972 we weren't ready, so I think in '76 there was better preparation going in."

Perreault was grateful to have the opportunity to shine for Team Canada in 1976. Having suffered because he was superfluous to the '72 squad, and again because of the reaction to his decision to go home early, he was doubly appreciative for the seasoning that he and Dionne now had behind them. "In 1976 we had more experience in the league. I was twenty-five years old and we were in our prime, whereas in '72 we were that much younger."

While Dionne and Perreault would enjoy higher profiles than in 1972, not all of Team Canada's players were as pleased with the shuffling of the deck. At training camp, Dionne took notice of Phil Esposito, who arrived ready to lead. "The Phil Esposito you saw in 1972 wasn't the same Phil Esposito you saw in 1976. I have tremendous respect for Phil, but by then he was in his declining years, and that is something we all have to go through. I remember at training camp I was playing with Danny Gare and Bobby Hull, and we were by far the best line. I had these two snipers, and I was feeding them, and Bobby was just—*swoosh*, one after another, into the net. Same with Danny. Now, Danny got a slight pull in his back, and the next day at practice—I remember we had black sweaters on—Phil came to Bob and me and said, 'If I don't play with you guys I won't be playing here at all.' There was no doubt in my mind that Danny deserved to be there, but politically, management was stuck. So Phil played with Bobby and me and it was, 'All right then, let's go!'

"That's one thing you get to know if you play with Phil. He's very opinionated and he gets to the point real quick. Like when he arrived at camp, I know that he asked how come his brother wasn't there. Well, if you're at the height of your career, you can call the shots. But Phil was no longer *the* guy. They made Bobby Clarke the captain and they tried to kind of push Phil aside. It was a different situation from '72—different people, and now Scotty Bowman was in charge."

Since his breakthrough performance in 1972, Bobby Clarke had established himself as a blue-chip player for the Philadelphia Flyers. Having recently won consecutive Stanley Cups, in '74 and

'75, and as leader of the popular, if not dominant, Flyers of the mid '70s, it was no surprise that Clarke was named captain of the Canada Cup squad. However, given a team loaded with future Hall of Famers and All-Stars in their prime, one might just as easily have drawn straws and come up with an equally fit selection.

Had it been up to Marcel Dionne, the choice would have been swiftly narrowed to one: for him, it was the "Golden Jet" all the way. "The guy that should have been captain was Bobby Hull. But he was still considered a traitor because he left the NHL. I'm always going to be thankful to him and the other guys that did that, going to the WHA. Regardless, here's a guy that scored all of those goals, racked up all those points, and they treated him like he was nonexistent. And Bobby wasn't the quietest guy, either. Believe me, the treatment he got with Team Canada '76 was cold. But again, him being there was a political thing because of the WHA. It was all about politics."

Hull had been blackballed from the 1972 Summit Series because of his decision to jump leagues. But despite any lingering resentment the NHL may have felt towards its exiled star, the organizers of Team Canada '76 bowed to the pressure to include him. To his credit, and to the disdain of the ill-intentioned hockey brass that would have banished him, Hull's play spoke volumes to all who witnessed the Golden Jet in his rightful place, competing for his country.

Peter Mahovlich, who played for Canada in '72, was delighted that Hull had been permitted to play in 1976. Like Dionne, he was fully impressed by what the veteran brought to the party. "The very first game, we didn't have a problem. We played in Ottawa against the Finns and we won pretty handily, 7–1 or 7–2 [Canada actually defeated Finland 11–2]. But the game where Hull stood out in my mind was in Toronto against Sweden and Borje Salming. I knew Bobby Hull was tough, and I knew he was a strong person and a courageous hockey player, but I had never seen him lay out a hit on someone. You know, like take the offensive and hit somebody. He was always the guy that others were trying to hit.

"That night, when Salming stepped onto the ice, he received cheers of appreciation for being a Maple Leaf. So on the very first shift Bobby Hull ran Borje Salming. He hit Salming with a great bodycheck—just levelled him. Well, Salming may have played for the Toronto Maple Leafs, but he was playing for Sweden now, and we were Team Canada. And that was the important thing. This is what we have to do. So Bobby Hull really set the tone for us. And I think it woke up the entire Gardens."

Team Canada had little trouble negotiating the round-robin portion of the tournament. The roster, which included no fewer than seventeen players on their way to the Hall of Fame, was tough to match. While some of the most efficient goal scorers of all time, including the likes of Dionne, Esposito and Hull (one of Bowman's many line combinations), suited up in the red and white of Team Canada, the defence was every bit as strong: Guy Lapointe, Denis Potvin, Larry Robinson and Serge Savard. Of course, there was one other blueliner who stood above the rest— and did so on a pair of bad knees.

"The whole series was Bobby Orr [who was named the tournament MVP]," Steve Shutt attests. "And we knew this was his last hurrah. Once it started, he never even practised. We never saw him. He was either in the clinic or he came out to play the game— and then he was gone. And the guy played great. I also think that he knew this was it, because from there he went to Chicago and played part of the year and then he was finished. I think that was really the inside story of that Canada Cup."

Rounding out Canada's strength at all positions was the biggest surprise of the tournament, goaltender Rogie Vachon. When Sam Pollock selected the team that Scotty Bowman and staff would coach, Vachon, who earned top-goalie laurels in the tournament, wasn't even on the initial list. "I think the four goalies that were invited to camp were Kenny Dryden, Gerry Cheevers, Chico Resch and Dan Bouchard," Vachon recalls. "I guess at the end of the Montreal Canadiens' season Dryden needed surgery. And I had played for the Montreal Canadiens under Sam Pollock when we won those Cups, so I guess that's how I came to be invited, sort of replacing Ken Dryden. When they gave me a chance, I got hot and I played all of the games."

Beyond its obvious wealth of talent, the key to the success of Team Canada was the adaptability of its players. While many were used to being the "go-to" men for their respective NHL clubs, each member of Team Canada settled into an unselfish style of play and focused keenly on his role. Steve Shutt became well acquainted with Dionne during the Canada Cup and discovered that unselfish quality in him.

"Marcel fit in with all of the players and was a good team man on and off the ice," Shutt recalls. "Sometimes in a situation like this, you don't know. You get guys that come in and they are stars from their teams, and egos come into play—and this can be a problem. You know, a guy like Marcel was probably playing close to thirty minutes a game in Los Angeles. Well, now he comes to the Canada Cup and he's got to play fifteen minutes. Some guys don't accept that very well—Marcel accepted it. And you never heard him complain; he was part of the team and he played well."

More than anything, Dionne was thrilled to have the opportunity and simply proceeded in his usual fashion. Knowing the strengths of his teammates was a skill he made use of his entire career. With Bowman's juggling of various line combinations in the tournament, Dionne would play to complement each player's style. For this reason, the centreman had tremendous success playing at right wing, flanking Phil Esposito and Bobby Hull.

"Basically, I understood how Bobby played the game. He was one of those guys who came off the wing," Marcel says. "Bobby would use the whole ice surface, but you've got to remember that some guys never did that. Some of the coaches we had would never let you leave the wing—it was just up and down. A centre could use the whole ice, but if you played on the wing they didn't want you going to the other side.

"So when Phil had the puck, I would watch Bobby. When Bobby would take off, I would just go to his side, and it worked very well—let him do whatever he wants. My role on that line was to get the puck to Phil and not worry about scoring. Bobby can do the scoring, and that's what happened. I would patch up the holes, and everything fell into place. It was great."

The only team that was able to muster a win against the Canadian powerhouse was Czechoslovakia. With an older goaltender named Vladimir Dzurilla having the outing of his career, the Czechs eked out a 1–0 victory that would help them earn a spot in the best-of-three final series against Canada.

Game one of the final resulted in a blowout: Team Canada trounced the Czechs, 6–0. Dzurilla, the hero from their first meeting, was pulled from the net after letting in four goals in the opening period. However, after Czech goalie Jiri Holecek gave up two goals in the next game, Dzurilla returned and played brilliantly. At the end of sixty minutes, the score was tied 4–4. Overtime would be needed to break the tie.

Because Canada was comfortably positioned with a win in hand, there was not the tension or desperation there had been in '72. Still, the final game of the 1976 Canada Cup tournament will be remembered as a hockey classic, due largely to the spectacular goaltending. While Dzurilla stood out for the Czechs, Vachon was even better. "Rogie was the goaltender that I enjoyed most over the years," Dionne says fondly. "He was sane. There always seemed to be something wrong with goalies. Imagine being in net, stopping pucks all day long. You had to be crazy. But Rogie was excellent. That Canada Cup was the best performance of his career."

While Vachon was called upon to make several big saves in the overtime period, it was a line change, made on a hunch by Scotty Bowman, that provided the finishing touches. "What happened on that goal, it was tied 4–4, and Scotty just comes up with this line. He said, 'Marcel, you go at centre with Darryl [Sittler] and Lanny [McDonald].'" Returning to their own end to help their defence clear the zone, the newly minted line immediately clicked. After McDonald directed the puck up to him, Marcel sent a breaking pass to Sittler, who gathered the puck and streaked down the left wing. As he crossed the blue line, Sittler faked a slap shot that froze Dzurilla, who was well out of his crease. Shifting to the outside, Sittler drove the puck into an open net, capping the game and the tournament.

Following the celebration of the goal, the two teams expressed their admiration for one another by exchanging sweaters. The swap was a spur-of-the-moment idea initiated by the happy-go-lucky Peter Mahovlich. Unfortunately for big Pete, the sentimental and monetary value of their Team Canada jerseys has skyrocketed with the increased popularity of sports memorabilia. Consequently, Mahovlich has had to bear the brunt of others' jibes for his kind gesture, especially from the one who will always be remembered for his swan-song performance.

"We had a comradeship with the Czechs because they were still in the grips of Russia at that time," he says. "They were trying to break away from Russia, and I felt that it was gesture of, you know, 'We're behind you guys.' We also have that common bond on the ice, where it doesn't matter what sweater you wear. But it's funny, because four or five years ago we were playing a golf tournament in Boston and I brought Bobby Orr this picture. It was of him going around the net with that Team Canada jersey on, just a beautiful picture—and he starts tearing into me." Mahovlich laughs. "He said, 'Geez, Pete, you know I would have liked to have kept that jersey.' I said, 'You know what? So would I!' What the hell was I thinking?!"

After the conclusion of the 1976 Canada Cup, Marcel Dionne and Rogie Vachon returned to the Los Angeles Kings with renewed confidence, ready to continue the building process that had brought Marcel to L.A. the year before. A new face would be joining them in 1976–77. Owner Jack Kent Cooke, aware of the premium that had lately been placed on rough play, wanted to make sure his team was equipped for that type of game and made an off-season acquisition.

As Marcel Dionne recalls, "It was 1976, I came to training camp from Team Canada and I walked into the dressing room and Pully was sitting on the bench. I took one look at him and said, 'What's the matter?' He said, 'We made a deal. We got Dave Schultz.' So again, Jack Kent Cooke had pulled off one of his nice deals. But this was the relationship I had developed with Pulford: now my coach was confiding in me. So I told him it was a good thing. I said, 'Pully, it's good for our team. He'll play for you. The toughest, baddest guy in the NHL is now playing for the Los Angeles Kings.'"

Without a doubt, Dave "The Hammer" Schultz was the genuine article when it came to tough customers. However, one might also say that he was nothing more than a goon, epitomizing the Philadelphia Flyers' notorious persona as the "Broad Street Bullies." Prior to his arrival in L.A., Schultz had led the league in penalty minutes in three of the last four seasons, amassing a staggering 472 penalty minutes in 1974–75. Nevertheless, Dionne saw the benefit of Schultz's strength, as did other appreciative Kings.

Glenn Goldup joined the team that same year and acknowledged the quality that made Schultz a contributing factor to consecutive Stanley Cups in Philadelphia. "Dave Schultz was good in that he brought a lot of toughness to our team. Before he arrived, there weren't many guys who could handle themselves. Apart from Dave Hutchison and Bert Wilson, L.A. had a lot of guys who couldn't punch their way out of a wet paper bag. But you know, when Schultz came, everybody wanted to know what the deal was with Philadelphia. Because there were tough teams, but in my opinion, that was the toughest team of all time. One night we had an exhibition game in Philadelphia and we couldn't even finish it—the ref called it off. There was no point. These guys were unbelievable. Even their fans were bad.

"So everybody wanted to know what that team was all about and what each guy was like individually. Well, as that Flyers team broke up, and all the players were gradually dispersed around the league, you found out that by themselves these guys were nothing. But collectively in Philly, Fred Shero had them so tight that it just seemed to work. And they all became better players as a result because they were given a little more room out there."

As with every teammate, Dionne saw Schultz's potential and hoped to maximize his ability to help the Kings win. Schultz's reputation alone allowed him more freedom on the ice than Marcel Dionne could ever dream of receiving. "Dave wanted to play," insists Dionne. "He lacked a few things, but he didn't have a bad shot. He would get down on himself and say, 'I'm just brutal.' But his brutal was better than most guys' brutal because he had more room. It was tough for him, adjusting to our team, because of the role he had in Philadelphia. Suddenly I'm playing with him and now he's in position, and geez, it's satisfying scoring goals instead of fighting all night. But he would do both. And I said to him, 'Are you crazy?' Still, I really enjoyed playing with Dave."

Schultz was sincere, as was his effort, both of which mattered a great deal in Dionne's book. At his best in the NHL, Dave Schultz achieved one twenty-goal season, the threshold often used as an indicator that a forward is of NHL calibre. In his first season with the Kings, Schultz managed half that total. However, it was not his soft hands that had got him to the NHL, nor was he expected to lead the Kings in scoring. He was there to provide a physical presence, to match the muscle that other teams were showing up with.

The rough side of the game didn't bother the Kings' star player. Dionne had faced it all along and would continue to do so, invitingly. Glenn Goldup remembers his grit: "Schultz's assignment wasn't to protect Marcel. It was the same as mine, to bring more toughness to the lineup, somebody that wouldn't back down. But Marcel never feared anyone. Guys would run into him and fall down. If you didn't bring the full load against Marce, you weren't going to knock him down. And on top of that, he'd make you look stupid if you tried to take advantage of him."

Since the departure of Dan Maloney, it had been left to other Kings to take up the physical slack. Having met his quota of pugilistic give-and-take for the team, Dave Hutchison was one of several teammates who noticed the extent to which Dionne held his own. And because Marcel would not look for help when it came to the rough stuff, his teammates—Hutchison among them—were even more inclined to show their support.

"I like Marcel a lot, and my feeling was that I wanted to stick up for him when guys would be running him," Hutchison confirms. "But Marcel was a tough player. I mean, for his size? I remember playing the Bruins in the playoffs back in 1976 and they had Terry O'Reilly, Wayne Cashman, Ken Hodge and all of those guys. So right off the bat, they're trying to get to Marcel because they know that he's the key to our team. As soon as the game started there was a scuffle, and I was in there, and of course Marcel was in the middle of it. These guys were taking shots at Marcel—and you know O'Reilly, he's saying, 'We're going to get you, Dionne, we're going to f—in' kill you, Dionne.'

"What Marcel did in response was one of the funniest things I've ever seen in all of sport. Marce turned around to them, took his finger and pressed it down on his nose and said, 'What are you going to do, break my nose?' Because you know that nose of his, you couldn't break it because it was already all over his f—in' face. Like it's been broken twelve times, and he just flattened it with his hand and said, 'What are you going to do, break my nose?'"

In a sport that has been criticized for being too violent, Dionne would certainly qualify as a player who has oft been on the receiving end of abuse. Based on his vast experience in this arena, Marcel easily discerns between dangerous behaviour and the need for enforcers. "What I would like people to understand is that there is a place for tough guys in the game of hockey. There is a place for Dave Schultz, Dave Hutchison and Tie Domi. And I know there are a lot of people who would banish these guys. But I respect these guys because they keep me honest. When they're in the game, I can't dance all night. If Wayne Gretzky and Mario Lemieux didn't like it, they were in the wrong game. And I'm not kidding; they didn't like to get hit.

"The tough guys aren't the ones that have been hurting the game. They're not. What's hurt our game has happened gradually over several years, and it started in minor hockey. Now, with the cages [face shields] they wear, because they are protected, the leagues let everything go that should be penalized. It's the introduction of cages that has built this up over the years. So when these players turn pro and remove their cages they're careless. The sticks don't come down. If you go and watch minor hockey or a college game, they do it over and over. But it's considered okay because they're wearing cages and nobody gets cut.

"That's the difference with the NHL today. In my day, you knew who the dirty players were and you kind of accepted it. Now, you've got the skilled players retaliating with high sticks and bad spearing; the frustration is out of control. My point is that the NHL is going to have to start policing itself and hockey is going to have to start changing. And that needs to get done in the early years of a hockey player's development."

In their second year in Los Angeles, Marcel and Carol moved their family of three from a rented house to one they bought in an outlying district called Rolling Hills Estates. Just as the Dionnes had had to adjust to the hockey culture in L.A., so too did the domestic life take some getting used to. "One night when we were in the new area, after we had gone to bed, we heard somebody walking on our roof," Carol says, continuing in a whisper: "I said, 'Marcel, somebody is trying to break in, they're on the roof.'

Marcel said, 'Nah.' Honest to God, it was so loud I was scared. I said, 'It sounds like two people. Go outside and check!'" Realizing that Carol's insistence was not about to let up, Marcel was forced to confront the intruders. "I'm wondering who could be on the roof making such a racket," Marcel says, then laughs. "They were peacocks! They would jump from roof to roof, house to house."

Vagrant peacocks aside, the distractions of Los Angeles were both numerous and tempting. Having heard about the pitfalls of the west coast lifestyle since the expansion of the league, Dionne made a concerted effort to maintain his focus on hockey. Again, because of the scrutiny he was under as the highest-paid King, even if he desired the charms of L.A., those things would have to wait. "When I came to L.A., for the first two years I didn't leave my house for anything other than hockey. Which means I didn't go to Disneyland, I didn't go to San Diego and I never went to Vegas. It was a total commitment to hockey. I had a pool, and I wouldn't swim. I didn't play tennis during the season and I didn't play golf—not even once!"

Even if Dionne had the inclination, the Kings' heavy travel schedule would have left him little energy to indulge in other activities. After spending what little free time he did have with his family, soon it was time to leave again. "When I look back on the years I was there, I realize that sometimes we were on the road for fifteen days. One time I was gone for twenty-one days, I came home for two days, and then had to leave for another four days for the All-Star Game. When I returned home, I was always so tired. I don't know how we did it. Today, they have charter flights that make all the difference. We never had that."

If nothing else, the trials of the west coast schedule provided memorable experiences that served to strengthen the bond of the Los Angeles players. From his inventory of amusing anecdotes, Glenn Goldup recounts how he and his roommate, Butch Goring, combated jet lag while deciding on a game-day meal.

"Heading west to east would just kill you. I remember this one time that we played in New York. We would have a morning skate and play that evening in Madison Square Garden. This one time, Butchy and I had missed the morning skate because we were just too tired, but it was optional anyway. So it was one in the afternoon and we're standing on the corner outside of our hotel, wondering what to do for a bite to eat, and Butchy goes, 'Ahh, I don't know, but we gotta eat something.' We looked down the street and there's a McDonald's townhouse. I'll never forget it. We had just woken up and down we went for a couple of Quarter Pounders, ate them and went back to bed.

"Shit, Butchy was too much. He had so many quirks. The best story about Butch was this one time when we were on a road trip to the Midwest. It was a quick one—three or four days out and then we'd pop back. Well, Butch shows up at the airport and he's got no luggage whatsoever, not even an overnight bag. He's wearing this blue corduroy suit and a white turtleneck.

"We're playing in Chicago that night, and all the way on the plane he's talking about these knackwursts that they've got at this one terminal in the Chicago airport. He says, 'We've got to go grab one of these knackwursts.' So we get off the plane and run down to this place and get a couple of big ones! We dig into them and Butchy blows a load of mustard for about eight inches down the front of his white turtleneck. Well, now he's stuck because he's got no luggage.

"Before long, we arrive at the rink and I'm in the dressing room waiting for him. I'm sitting there laughing because I've already told Murph—I said, 'Wait until you see this.' So Butch walks in, blue corduroy suit, white turtleneck—no stain! Murph and I look at each other and we're like, 'I don't get it.' Butch walks over to his stall, takes his jacket off, and there's the stain—down the back! All he did was turn it around. We had a lot of fun."

As was the case with most players, Dionne loved the bonding experiences that made a team a tight bunch. In support of this approach, Marcel had extended an open invitation to his home to all of his teammates. However, with Los Angeles being such a sprawling city, and Marcel having a house that was relatively out of the way for most teammates, impromptu visits were less frequent than he would have liked. One player who did make the effort was Glenn Goldup.

"Marce was one of the nicest guys you could ever meet. He used to say stuff like, 'I always invite people over to my house and nobody ever comes. My house is open to you guys *anytime* you want—you guys think I'm stuck up.' So he was going on like this one day and we were all laughing. And I was pretty good at stirring up the pot. Amongst Marce, Murph and Butchy, I'd get 'em going really good.

"So one morning I figure, 'All right, I'll show him.' I showed up at his door at 7:30 in the morning before practice. I'm ringing the doorbell and I get him out of bed. He comes down yelling, 'What the heck is going on?' After he settled down he got Carol up—Lisa was just a baby at the time. Next thing you know, Carol is making breakfast and we're sitting down together. For about a year after that he'd always say to the team, 'Goldie's the only one who comes to my house—even if it's at 7:30 in the morning, he's the only guy who shows up!' But Marce was very proud of that stuff. Literally, he got the entire household up so we could have breakfast together. So he held true to his word, even though I arrived at 7:30 a.m."

Overall, the camaraderie amongst the Kings was quite good—at least for the players. The awkward conditions that Bob Pulford and Jake Milford experienced under Jack Kent Cooke still existed. However, for much of the 1976–77 season, the breakdown of Cooke's marriage distanced him from the hockey operations in L.A., which improved the day-to-day environment for management. For Dionne, the 1976–77 season would stand as a new personal best as he achieved the first of six 50-goal seasons. With his contribution of 53 goals and 69 assists, Marcel also attained his highest point total ever (122) and erased any concerns once expressed by the Kings owner.

Dionne's tight focus on hockey continued to pay off. While he did enjoy the diverse character of his team, he understood that his level of dedication would differ from that of his teammates. Still known to lead by example and challenge others to be their best, he never imposed his approach on any one player. In return, he wished that he would receive the same consideration. While attending a Kings team party with Carol, Marcel realized, to his disappointment, that something he wanted no part of was a casual indulgence for several of the L.A. players.

"It was at Dave Schultz's house," recalls Carol Dionne. "Everybody had been drinking, and it was two or three in the morning. Somebody asked Dave's wife if he could smoke and she said, 'Fine.' Marcel didn't see it right away."

"I was having a great time. Then I saw some of them passing this joint around and I got the impression by how relaxed they were that it wasn't the first time," Dionne says. "Well, I was devastated. I said, 'I can't believe you guys.' They should have told me and I would have left, which is what I did. I said, 'F— these assholes!' I was mad, I was drunk, and I slammed the door on the way out.

"I've never done drugs. I've tried to recall if I've ever smoked a joint, and I have no recollection of doing it, there's no way. If I did, I must have been drinking. But when we went to Los Angeles it was obvious, and I just didn't want to be part of that scene. Later on, we went to a few of those L.A. movie premiere parties and that's when the cocaine started to come around. I have never seen cocaine, per se—like to be in a room with it—but you'd know what was going on, that you're not part of the scene and they'd be waiting for you to leave. At training camp, the NHL would warn you. The league security would come and tell you not to get involved with drugs. But some players ignored that."

Recalling the incident at the team party, Glenn Goldup revealed some of the wisdom he's acquired over the years. "That was my fault at Schultzy's place. You know what, we were having a good time and I lit one up and Marcel was very upset. Absolutely—*very* upset. He grabbed Carol and they left. And I felt very bad after that happened. I learned a lesson that day, I really did. You have to be sensitive to other people and other people's situations, and other people's feelings.

"I was never a great hockey player. Hockey was really of no benefit to me in my life, other than it taught me a lot of lessons. I think hockey better prepared me for my life today, more than it did for what was going on back then. At the time, you're laughing and being stupid. But afterwards, when I thought about it—and I'm talking years and years later—it just wasn't right. I never resented Marcel for his reaction. He did what he had to do, and what I did was wrong. You just can't do that to people. If that's the way you are, then fine. But don't put it in front of other people and put them in a situation where they can be tied to it."

The day after the party, Dionne received a visit from Dave Schultz, who apologized for the circumstances that caused Marcel to leave his house in a fury. While Marcel appreciated Schultz for shouldering the responsibility, he was still left with a clouded mood that required some reflection. The reality that several of his teammates had a drastically different notion of what commitment to the game meant was something he had to accommodate in his stand towards casual drug use.

"If someone says it's okay to smoke a joint, then that's their opinion," Marcel says. "I conducted myself according to what the law says. I've always been chicken shit when it comes to the law. If that's what they say the law is, then that's what I go by. But let me tell you, I learned from that experience. I grew up quite a bit. I know my life is filled with a lot of wonderful things, and I'm sure passing a joint isn't the end of the world. But I came to realize that I have a healthy body and my highs are natural highs. When it comes to how others conduct themselves, I can't have everything my way. So I guess I just resolved to block it out of my mind, which was one way to deal with it. And even though I could see that certain guys were going down, I tried not to judge them.

"The way I look at it today, with my own kids, is with an understanding that they will try drugs. What I believe is more important is what we do about it. With the ones that try it and move on, it's okay. But what about the kids that become addicted to drugs? What are we doing for them? In my opinion, we spend so much money trying to educate people about the dangers of drugs. Where I would like there to be more focus is on the ones that are really addicted. They're the ones we should be trying to save."

Chapter Nine

"**J**ACK KENT COOKE was the hands-on owner to end all hands-on owners," reports Bob Miller. "He was involved in every aspect of the game. Before I arrived in L.A., during the first few years of the team, I understood that he would take his skates to training camp and go out on the ice and try to score on Terry Sawchuk. And Sawchuk would let him score just so Cooke could say that he scored on the great Terry Sawchuk.

"I must say that I admired the fact that he was a self-made multi-multi-millionaire. He was almost a billionaire when he died. He started out selling encyclopedias in Canada; he'd tell a story of selling encyclopedias out in Saskatchewan right after he'd been married, and he didn't have enough money to buy dinner for himself and his wife. So this one night he found the house of this high school principal and got him to put down a five-dollar deposit on a set of encyclopedias. And that's what they used to buy dinner that night."

To appreciate how difficult it was to work under this self-made man, one only has to speak to someone in his employ when he owned the Kings. Team broadcaster Bob Miller offers highlights from the volatile reign.

"I'll never forget the time that Jack Kent Cooke called me into his office, along with my broadcast partner at the time, and said, 'I want to run thirteen 30-second commercials per period.' I said, 'Mr. Cooke, I don't think we could ever get that many commercials in.' Back in those days, they weren't stopping the games for commercials, so you had to get them in whenever you could. And I said, 'We're currently running four, and some nights, depending on the pace of the game, it's tough to get even four in.' So he said,

'Well, then, you will mention the sponsor during the play-by-play.' And Datsun was our main sponsor at the time—they're now called Nissan. He said, 'For instance, you will say, "There goes Marcel Dionne scooting down the ice like a Datsun!"' And he said to me, 'What do you think of that?' I couldn't believe my ears. I said, 'Mr. Cooke, I can't imagine saying that once, let alone eighty times a year.' He went berserk. He screamed at me, 'Do you know how many people want your job? And they're this close to getting it! Get out of my sight.' He was just screaming, and when I came out of his office, the secretary, who was ninety feet down the hall, said, '*What* did you do?'

"So Cooke told me to get out of his sight and return at two o'clock, and I had better have some answers as to how I was going to do this. My partner Dan Avey and I were laughing after the meeting because he was in there with me while Cooke was just screaming at me. And Dan said to me, 'Are we fired?' I said, 'Not until two o'clock, and it's only a quarter to twelve, so we've got a couple of hours.' Then we began kidding around. I said, 'Dan, how about this: if the Kings score, like, fifteen seconds after the opening face-off, I'll say, "The Kings have scored at the fifteen-second mark," and you holler, "Dat-*soon*, Dat-*soon*?!"' So we were laughing, but then realized that we had better come up with something or we would be gone.

"When I went back to see Mr. Cooke he said, 'Well?' And I said, 'Well, Mr. Cooke, we could say, "The play has stopped, and on the Datsun scoreboard the Kings lead Chicago, 2–1." Or we could say, "We'll be back in a moment. This is the Datsun Kings radio broadcast."' And he looked at me and said, 'My, my, my—aren't you a brilliant fellow?' Really condescending. So, he thought that would be fine and we were dismissed and that was the end of that.

"Another thing he used to do was call us while we were on the air. The phone would ring and if we hadn't mentioned season's tickets in a while he would just be screaming at us—during the play-by-play! I remember one night Dan Avey took the call and slammed the phone down and just got up and left. I thought he had quit right in the middle of the broadcast, he was so upset.

"Regarding Cooke's constant phoning, I tell people that I got to be like Pavlov's dog. You know the experiment where he rang a bell and fed the dog, and then every time the dog heard a bell he'd start salivating, thinking he was going to be fed? I was like Pavlov's dog: anytime I'd hear a phone ring, I'd say, 'Don't forget season's tickets are available.' It wouldn't even have to be the phone next to me. It would be somewhere else in the press box and I would do a season's tickets plug.

"Jack Kent Cooke was tough to work for, there's no doubt about that. I worked for him for six years and the only reason I made it was that for four of those six years he was out of town tending to other business."

At the conclusion of the 1976–77 season Marcel Dionne felt sufficiently established in Los Angeles that he allowed himself to indulge in the odd game of golf during the off-season. He had been doing just that with a few teammates when they decided to address what they were hearing from the rumour mill about their coach. The talk was that the same autocratic boss that drove Bob Miller up the wall had now inspired the Kings' coach, Bob Pulford, as well as general manager Jake Milford, to seek work with other hockey clubs. For Dionne, the loss of such sound minds amounted to a squandering of resources that the young Kings franchise could ill afford. If it could make a difference in Pulford's decision, Dionne wanted to show that he was behind their coach.

"I was with a couple of players—we had just played golf—and we ended up at Bob Pulford's house. We wanted to find out what was going on, and when we realized he was [leaving], I couldn't believe it. I remember saying, 'Bob, you can't leave.' I mean, I had finally started to see my hockey career and life on track. We had two good playoff series with Boston and Atlanta. So I asked him if he was going to stay with us, but the deal was already done. He wouldn't say anything about it, but I knew he was gone.

"I was lucky to have two years with Bob before he signed with Chicago. I think he came to realize, after watching me for a year, that there *were* certain things I could really help the team with. And he began to take advantage of those things, like on the power play. He would play me on the point, and I would play the entire power play. Or we'd be down a goal, playing short-handed, and he would come down the bench and tell me, 'If you get an opportunity, I want you to go for it.' You know how much that means to a player? So I really felt good playing for Bob. I can honestly say that Bob Pulford was never a topic amongst the players after a game, in terms of questioning the moves he made. When he was gone, I kind of lost hope and realized that my experience in Los Angeles would become one of survival."

Towards the end of Cooke's soured ownership of the Kings franchise, he became less and less of a hands-on owner and relocated to Nevada. "He was hiding from his wife in Nevada because he had just separated from her," says Glenn Goldup, who once dealt with a similar predicament, albeit on a much smaller scale. "California law, as far as divorces go, is expensive—and I know from firsthand experience. It was bad, and it cost the guy at that time. So he went to Las Vegas; as long as he was there, she couldn't subpoena him to court and nail him for whatever. It was a way for him to position himself to make a deal."

Eventually, Cooke's dissatisfaction with the Kings would result not only in the loss of the coach and GM, but in the sale of the team. Ron Stewart and George Maguire would follow as replacements for Pulford and Milford respectively. After one season, Stewart was replaced by Bob Berry for 1978–79, which was also Cooke's last year as owner of the Los Angeles Kings.

Three different coaches in as many years reflected the unstable situation in L.A. as well as any other lacklustre statistic could. Nevertheless, Dionne's most memorable story from this period of

continuous upheaval is told with present-day good humour—
despite its deadly serious nature. "We were in Pittsburgh and I got
a phone call. My roommate was Danny Grant; he answered the
phone and said to me, 'Marcel, there's a Roger from California
that would like to speak to you.' It was early in the morning and I
said, 'Danny, I don't know any Roger from California.' I picked
up the phone and said, 'Hello?' The voice on the other end said,
'Listen, I've got a high-powered rifle and if you score a goal
tonight I'm going to blow your f—in' head off!' And he hung up
the phone. I told Danny Grant, 'You're not going to believe this,
but the guy that just called said that if I play or score tonight he's
going to blow my head off.'

"I remember that after the call I was uncertain if he had said
'play' or 'score'. Anyway, Danny started to laugh a little and told
me not to worry about it, but I was concerned. It was the first time
I had ever experienced something like this. Our room was up
around the tenth floor of our hotel, so then Danny started mess-
ing with me. He slid out of the bed and crawled across the floor to
the wall of the room. Then he got up and inched his way around
the room with his back pressed up against the wall until he
reached the curtains. Danny was laughing while he peeked out the
window and said, 'I don't see any snipers.' Well, I was laughing,
too, but I was like, 'Hey, get off my back!'

"To be on the safe side, I thought I should inform our coach,
Bob Berry, about what had happened. Bob told NHL security,
and a guy from NHL security called me and said, 'Marcel, I
wouldn't worry too much about it. We'll have people there
tonight.' Then I asked what the chances were of this guy being for
real. He said, 'Well, actually there could be a chance, maybe one
in a million.' Well, that's all he needed to say. I wanted to hear that
there was no chance whatsoever!

"As we entered the Igloo [Pittsburgh's Civic Arena], it was
weighing on my mind. So now we're in the warmup and I can't
stop thinking about it. And I was a guy who always skated slowly
in the warmup—you know, take it easy and get warmed up. On

that night I was skating like crazy, weaving in and out of everybody. The entire time, I was thinking that some lunatic had a rifle with a scope on me and he wants to nail me. I was ducking and weaving around guys. The warmup was eighteen minutes and I stayed out there for about ten.

"When the national anthem started, I was really concerned. I was relieved that I wasn't in the starting lineup because I would have been an easy target right there on the blue line. I was on the bench for the anthem and I thought, 'Well, now he's got me, because I'm standing still.' So I started to move, rocking back and forth. Bob Berry was near me on the bench and he could see my anxiety. He came over and said, 'Don't worry, I'm with you tonight.' Well, I looked at him and said, 'Sure you're with me, but what if he misses me, then he hits you?' Then he took off right away. He was joking, and we both laughed, he more so than I.

"So the game got under way, and what happened was [Dave] Taylor, [Charlie] Simmer and I were on the ice, and I ended up with the puck, looking at an open net. All I had to do was tap it in. For maybe a half a second I paused, not wanting to score, but I put it in and quickly skated over to the guys to celebrate. I thought that in a pack of tall players a sniper wouldn't be able to get a clear shot at me."

At this point in the 1978–79 season Charlie Simmer was getting his second crack at making the Kings lineup. Simmer remembers the team being briefed before the game and the manner in which Marcel's teammates helped him get through that night. "It was just a regular-season game, and Pittsburgh was really not that hot of a team. But the FBI and security checked it all out, and they assured us that it was probably a hoax. So everybody was kidding Marcel and having a good time with it. And Marcel did score a goal." Simmer laughs. "Of course, there was a funny unwritten rule that you tried to sit beside the guy on the bench who just scored a goal or who had a good shift because you'd get on TV and that way you'd get more exposure. That was the only occasion when no one wanted to sit next to Marcel for the entire game."

Although the death threat turned out to be nothing more than a hoax, the torment was a very trying experience psychologically. It was one of the unfortunate aspects of life as a celebrity athlete.

The next time the Kings returned to Pittsburgh, security took the precaution of screening all of the team's telephone calls. Wisely, Dionne put the experience behind him and approached the game as he would any other. And while he had forgotten about the sniper, he quickly discovered after netting an early goal that his teammates had not. "When I got that goal I turned around and there was nobody there to celebrate with. They all skated over to our bench, right away. It really wasn't on my mind, but they all remembered and had a good laugh." Marcel jabs, "Now I tell that story when I speak at various functions and I use the line, 'We never played as a team because nobody wanted to die as a team.'"

As the seventies wound down the L.A. Kings survived with a modicum of hope, if not reasonable promise. Although the Kings' All-Star goaltender Rogie Vachon had been traded to the Detroit Red Wings, Dionne was now in his prime and continued to raise the game of the players around him. Near the top of that list was Butch Goring. In the four seasons prior to Dionne's arrival Goring had scored 21, 28, 28 and 27 goals. With Dionne as a teammate, Goring's numbers jumped to 33, 30, 37 and 36. Dionne knew of Goring's potential and wished he would tap it. "I tried to push Butch, because I knew he could do it. But he would say, 'I don't want to score too many this year because they'll want even more next year.' Christ, I hated that!"

The loss of Goring to the New York Islanders in the latter part of the 1979–80 campaign was one of many changes that occurred in L.A. that season. To Goring's delight, he would play a key role in helping the Islanders win four consecutive Stanley Cups. Goring's departure would be more than compensated for, however, by the emergence of the most efficient offensive unit the game had yet seen: the Triple Crown Line.

The unit consisted of Marcel Dionne, Dave Taylor and Charlie Simmer. Of the two wingers, Taylor had been first to earn his spot next to Marcel. "The first half of that [1977–78] season, I just kind of kicked around on the fourth line and got scratched the odd time. About halfway through the year, I got an opportunity to play with Marcel, and we just seemed to click. We had some chemistry. I think our first game was on the road against Pittsburgh; we scored a couple of goals and we ended up winning the game. And that was it for me. I was Marcel's right winger from that point forward.

"He virtually ignited my career. It was an opportunity to play with, you know, one of the top five offensive players in the game. And because of that I got a lot of ice time. I got a lot of ice time on the power play, and we played together killing penalties. That was really what launched my career."

While Dionne and Taylor were establishing a rapport with the Kings, Simmer was trying simply to establish that he belonged in the NHL. Drafted by the California Golden Seals in 1974 (they were to become the Cleveland Barons two years later), he spent three seasons shuttling between the big league and the organization's farm team in Salt Lake City. Unable to crack the lineup of one of the least distinguished franchises in NHL history, Simmer began to seriously question his ability to make a go of it in the majors. In 1977, he signed as a free agent with the Kings, only to spend almost the entire season with Springfield of the American League. But during the 1978–79 season, Bob Berry's first as coach in L.A., Simmer finally got the break that would see him hit his professional stride.

"My coach in the minors before I made it in L.A. was Bob Berry. I made the All-Star Team in the American league, had a good year and I just really worked hard that summer," Simmer recalls. "I figured the next season would be my last chance, being my fifth year as a pro. Then Bob Berry was named head coach of the Los Angeles Kings and I knew this was my best chance. Unfortunately, I went to camp and I was the only guy on a two-way contract, so Bob sent me down.

"When I got called up I wasn't having the greatest year and I thought, 'Well, am I going back to the pulp and paper mill in

Terrace Bay, Ontario, or should I go to Europe?' I had three months to ride out, and I had some friends in Europe, so I figured I might try that. Basically, I was three months away from quitting hockey.

"It was January 12, 1979, when Bob Berry called. The [Kings were] in Detroit and then on their way to Boston before they would return to L.A. Again, I figured I'd get called up, sit on the bench, play a couple shifts, and then, 'You didn't show us much; you're going back down.' That's basically the way it was back then, especially for me being in my fifth year. When I went to Detroit, it was the old Olympia, which was kind of neat. I said, 'Okay, Bob, where do you want me to sit?'—that type of thing. And he surprised me and said, 'You're going to play with Marcel and Davey. We've tried everybody—Danny Grant, Murray Wilson, Glenn Goldup. It's your job until you lose it.'

"So we went into Detroit and beat them on January 13—I still remember the date—and Marce got three or four goals, which was just textbook for him any time he went back to Detroit. You just knew he was going to get points. Davey also ended up getting a couple of points, and I ended up with nothing. Then it was off to Boston, where we beat the Bruins and I got an assist or two but didn't score. And I had some friends drive up from where I was playing in nearby Springfield so they could drive me back," Simmer laughs. "Because I really didn't have a lot of confidence at that point.

"After the game, Bob came in and started talking with me. He said, 'You've got to go back to Springfield,' which is what I expected. And then he kind of laughed and said, 'I need you to pick up some clothes and come back out with us.' As he joked, he said, 'I've made two mistakes coaching this year: sending you down to the minors and not calling you up soon enough.' We had 38 games left in the season and I finished out the year with the Kings—but that's how close I was to quitting."

Playing with Dionne and Taylor, Simmer secured his position with the club scoring 21 goals and 27 assists in the remaining

38 games. As it turned out, the era of the Triple Crown Line was being ushered in just as another chapter in team history was about to close, as Jack Kent Cooke sold the club. Simmer recalls his one and only encounter with the old boss. "It was at the end of the season, the year I got called up for good. We were sitting in the locker room at the end of our last game. We'd just lost in the playoffs, and this tiny little man comes walking into the locker room. I'd never met him and really didn't realize who the owner was. I'd probably heard his name, Jack Kent Cooke, but I didn't associate the owner with the team because we'd never met. And I never had any correspondence with him, nor had I seen a picture of him up until that point.

"So this guy came into our dressing room and he gave a big ol' speech on how next year was going to be better, the team was going to be stronger and so on. And then he just walked out. I looked at Davey, who dressed beside me, and said, 'Well—who the hell was that?' He just laughed and said, 'That's the owner of the team.' But ultimately, that spring, Jack Kent Cooke sold the team to Jerry Buss."

Having hailed from Canada, the birthplace of hockey, Cooke believed he could bring hockey to sunny California and see the sport flourish. Cooke had made the assumption that, with 200,000 transplanted Canadians living in the greater Los Angeles area, hockey would take off like a rocket. Twelve years of disappointing attendance later, the Kings' owner had changed his mind. Cooke's famous lament was that the 200,000 Canadians must have moved to California because they hated the sport of hockey.

Ironically, Cooke's farewell remarks would prove prophetic. In their first year under Buss's ownership, the Kings had a banner year. As the Triple Crown Line proceeded to burn through the league, Simmer, who had been contemplating a job at the mill less than a year before, would lead the league with 56 goals. Of even greater significance was the career season that Marcel Dionne embarked upon.

Dionne was pleased with the changing of the guard in the

owner's suite. Whatever passion Cooke had had for hockey, by the end of his days with the Kings it was long gone. Marcel felt that a new boss, and a new bankroll, could only improve the overall situation. "I think everybody was excited. Now we had new blood, somebody that was going to spend money on the team. You know, Jerry Buss liked hockey—he didn't understand hockey, but he liked hockey—and that was the main thing."

For his part, Dionne would not only earn the confidence of the Kings' new head honcho that season, but in so doing he would unequivocally establish himself as the best player in the league. While his contemporary Guy Lafleur had been bolstering his résumé by winning Stanley Cups and scoring titles in Montreal, Dionne had been excelling quietly with little support in Los Angeles. However, in order to secure his due recognition, he would have to prevail in a neck-and-neck scoring race with the future of hockey, Wayne Gretzky.

It was a year of great significance in the NHL as the mighty Montreal Canadiens dynasty of the 1970s gave way to the New York Islanders powerhouse of the early '80s. The league had also grown from seventeen teams to twenty-one after absorbing four survivors of the defunct World Hockey Association. Gretzky, who turned pro at seventeen, had been one of the WHA's brightest stars in its final season, and he hit the ground running in his debut NHL season, engaging the veteran Dionne in a year-long duel for the Art Ross Trophy. Gretzky, also known as "The Great One," would go on to dominate the NHL, and rewrite its record books, for the next decade and then some. However, in the spring of 1980 it was Marcel Dionne who stood atop the game's summit.

As a team, the Kings finished second in their division. Dave Taylor registered 37 goals and 53 assists for 90 points, while Charlie Simmer contributed 56 goals and 45 assists for 101 points. Marcel Dionne's 53 goals and 84 assists, for a league-leading 137 points, tied Wayne Gretzky's combination of 51 goals and 86 assists. But because he had scored more goals, Dionne was awarded the Art Ross Trophy as the NHL's most prolific scorer.

Prior to this achievement, Dionne had been acknowledged for his skill and sportsmanship, having been presented with the Lady Byng Trophy on two separate occasions (1975 and 1977). But more than his gentlemanly play, it was Dionne's desire that consistently placed him amongst the elite talent in the NHL.

Bob Miller remembers Dionne's competitive fire. "I have never seen another player like Dionne. He would get the puck and come down the ice and I would bet you my house that he was going to score. I talked to Jimmy Fox, my broadcasting partner now, who played ten years for the Kings, and Jimmy said, 'I have never seen a stronger player than Marcel Dionne. He would go to the net and people would be breaking sticks over him and it wouldn't stop him. He had that kind of determination.'

"Marcel was short and stocky and had a low centre of gravity. You couldn't knock him down or get him off balance. And he had that determination. I remember a conversation with Marcel, he said, 'I've always told players, even if it's an empty net, shoot that puck like you're going to drive it through the back of the netting. Don't ever let up. Because the moment you let up, something happens. The shot gets deflected or the goalie makes the save.' He said, 'I don't care if I'm five feet in front of an empty net, I just blast it.' And that's the way the great goal scorers were."

After the Kings' exceptional year, Marcel Dionne was filled with a renewed enthusiasm. The fact that Bob Berry was kept on as head coach was the first sign of management stability that the Kings had seen in four years. Dionne also appreciated that Berry tried to raise the level of professionalism in the relaxed Kings' dressing room. Charlie Simmer recalls, "As talented and as gifted as Marcel was, if the effort wasn't there from his teammates, he really was frustrated. He was the leader and the person that was most associated with the L.A. Kings. I remember that Bob Berry instituted a 'tan rule,' whereby you would be fined depending on how deep your tan was—for sunburns, things like that. It was monetary, but not a lot of money—especially compared to what players make today. But guys from different teams would always ask, 'Did you really have a tan rule?' Basically, the idea was that if you showed up fully sunburned, you weren't going to feel good about it. In around 1980 and '81 the Kings held on to their draft picks, which was a rarity, and we ended up with Jimmy Fox, Jay Wells, Larry Murphy, Greg Terrion and Dean Hopkins. They were very young players, so really the rules were meant to help those guys stay focused."

As a veteran and a leader, Mike Murphy concurred with the directive to rein in the laid-back approach. "Bob Berry didn't want the guys wearing shorts to practice, and he was justified in his thinking. If you get up in the morning and the first thing you do is throw on a pair of cutoffs and a T-shirt, and you go to the rink looking like a bum, you've given no thought to getting dressed and no thought to preparing for practice. So his theory was to dress relatively neat, so you had to wear pants and a shirt. And it wasn't a bad idea.

"But Marcel handled all of that very well because he was a true professional. He prepared well, he conditioned well and he performed well. If you weren't as mentally strong as Marcel was, you could get sidetracked by a lot of things that were happening. Take your pick: the nice weather, the pools, the parties, the golf, any number of ways you could spend your time outdoors doing various activities. There were a lot of distractions. And there is a huge movie industry there. You've got the movie people around; you've got the television shows that are shot there. So there's a lot of side issues that came into play if you played for the L.A. Kings."

Having become more accustomed to a hockey milieu where it wasn't unusual to lace up for practice alongside, say, Glenn Frey of the Eagles, Marcel was able to establish a balance, if not a buffer zone, between his approach and the lifestyles of those around him. As a polar opposite to Dionne, no player was more thorough in exploring the California experience than the one

Marcel and his teammates fittingly and affectionately referred to as Goldie.

Glenn Goldup beams when he recalls the heady days in California, "First of all, it was the whole mystique of California. For me, it was the first time I saw the west coast, the ocean; as soon as I got into town I drove right to the coast and it was unbelievable. It was like a magnet. I couldn't believe it. There I was, standing by the Pacific Ocean, something that we Torontonians and Canadians from the east coast dream about because it's Hollywood and the whole bit.

"So I got down there and I tried to eat up as much of it as I could outside of hockey—and it was a distraction. It's very demanding; I mean the nightlife of Sunset Boulevard, Beverly Hills, the beaches. Eventually, my marriage went downhill, my hockey went downhill, everything went downhill. But my nightlife and lifestyle around L.A. were fantastic! It was fast, it was happening. I was rubbing shoulders with everybody, playing golf all summer long with people like Alice Cooper, Evel Knievel, Mac Davis. It was a pretty interesting time.

"I had a Mercedes 450 SL, a yellow one; rode with the top down all the time. And after practice I'd jump on my motorcycle and go up the coast, up U.S. 101, along the coastal highway. At one time, for three weeks in a row I rode motorcycles with Steve McQueen in Malibu. I met him there. I was pulled over and I realized who he was and we got chatting and he showed a little interest in hockey. I said to him, 'I saw your Indian coming in here. I've got my motorcycle outside; let's go for a tool.' And away we went.

"At the end of the run I had to go back down into the Valley, in Valencia, and I said, 'If you're interested, I'll meet you back here next week, on Thursday.' And two weeks in a row I came back and rode motorcycles with Steve McQueen. When I went back to meet him the fourth time, he wasn't there. About three weeks later there was an article in the newspaper that he was in Mexico for cancer treatment. So that was the last I saw of him. We went for a bike ride, and then I left him and waved goodbye. That was very cool."

Throughout the 1970s, the L.A.–based Eagles were amongst the most popular and most commercially successful bands. As a result both of circumstance and mutual interest, it wasn't long before they and the Kings bonded.

Dave Hutchison remembers striking up a friendship with Glenn Frey. "Glenn Frey is from Detroit originally, that's his hometown. He grew up watching the Red Wings and *Hockey Night in Canada*; he could get *Hockey Night in Canada* off his aerial as a kid. So hockey was his favourite sport. When he became wealthy and famous out in L.A. with the Eagles, he was a season's ticket holder at the Kings games.

"I met Glenn because I had long hair back then. Bob Nevin and I were the two single guys on the Kings, living together, and we would go up to the bar, the Forum Club, after games, even though we weren't supposed to. Now, Pully was our coach at the time and he didn't want us going there because after games people are drinking and if we lost, people could say something—'Hey, ya f—in' bum,' or whatever, you know. So he didn't want us going in there, but Nevy and I used to sneak in. And that's when I ran into Glenn Frey. He came up and introduced himself, and of course he had the long hair and the moustache. This was just before the album *One of These Nights* came out. Anyway, Glenn and I kind of struck up a little friendship, and he was a big Kings fan. The Eagles would be on the road and he would be out there playing with a Kings jersey on.

"Later on, I got suspended and Marcel was out of the lineup for a few days. When the team went on the road, if you were injured or suspended you didn't go. We'd stay home and practise at the Culver City arena, the old practice rink we had. So I used to bring Glenn along, and that's where he skated with Marce and myself. He loved to play hockey and would show up religiously, and at the same time he's recording these albums. He would get home at three o'clock in the morning, shit-faced and stoned, and then show up at our practice rink at eight o'clock in the morning—still all googly-eyed—and he'd come out and play with us. He wasn't an NHLer, but he grew up in Detroit skating. So he'd come out and play, sweat like a bastard, and then go back to making his music."

Whenever the Eagles played the Fabulous Forum—the home of the Kings—all of the hockey players and their dates would occupy an entire section at the front of the stage. But as Hutchison points out, and Mike Murphy confirms, the team and the musicians enjoyed a unique friendship that extended beyond rubbing shoulders at the odd concert. "Occasionally, we'd go to restaurants together after games—they'd come with us or we'd go off with them. We also played baseball against each other," Murphy says. "It was called 'the Jocks versus the Junkies.' This was back in the '70s, when times were a little different. A few of the players still keep up with some of them. I know that Glenn Frey ran into Dave Taylor a couple of months ago, and he asked Dave how Hutchie was, how Marcel was, how Murph was—you know, how are the guys doing?"

If southern California in the 1970s was renowned for a decadent lifestyle that Marcel managed to steer clear of, the Kings' new owner, Jerry Buss, personified that image. And depending on your outlook, that could be seen as a detriment to the team's success or a green light for the players to pull into the L.A. fast lane. Dionne didn't count himself amongst those who might have thought Buss's swinging style was befitting of an NHL owner. "Dr. Jerry Buss would come in wearing blue jeans, no tie, silk shirt and was always visible with all of his young chicks—that was his big thing—and to party. But all of that died real quick for me. Maybe some guys were impressed, but I was not impressed at all."

Without a doubt, Marcel's degree of self-discipline was on another level from that of his teammates. Certainly, most of the younger players had no problem with the company that Buss kept. More to the point, at that time many of the Kings were on the same page. "We had ten or eleven single guys living on the beach," Charlie Simmer observes, "and that lead to a lot of distraction. That was something Marcel really tried to put his foot down on. And when he did, he was labelled as a moody, grumpy player.

"In the dressing room he'd always have the corner stall, off to the one side, and that was his domain." Asked to recall who sat next to Dionne, Simmer laughs. "Nobody wanted to; there was a revolving door over in that corner. Davey and I were real close to him—maybe one stall over to the right. Mike Murphy was over there for a while, but after that it was just a lot of young players. Basically, it was because at the end of each game all of the media wanted to talk to Marcel. You couldn't stick a veteran beside him, because all of the media would be there and the guy beside him couldn't change to get out of there. So it was, 'Let's stick a rookie in there.' And the rookie would be shaking in his boots all year.

"But I think the distractions affected a lot of players. I myself found it very easy to play there. There were a lot of Hollywood people at the games—Jerry Buss was very good about bringing all of his guests down to the locker room. You'd meet all kinds of different people, like Michael Douglas, Hal Linden—of course, there weren't as many as when Wayne Gretzky arrived.

"And anytime there were parties in Hollywood, you were invited to go up to them. It was just astronomical for a kid from Terrace Bay to look at these houses. I mean, some of these homes were bigger than the mill in Terrace Bay. I remember Jerry Buss had a birthday party for his business partner, and it lasted three days! One night it was up in Bel Air at the big house, another of the nights was down in Malibu at the beach house. You just showed up and whatever you wanted was there—all paid for. They had a gambling night, with funny money, and the person with the most money at the end of the night won a two-week vacation in Paris. It was just amazing. And of course Jerry was always one to have younger beautiful women around him at all times. It was just, like, wow!

"It was kind of amazing for someone playing there that these distractions existed, and yet you didn't have the pressure of winning and losing like you would in Philadelphia or Toronto. I

Dionne motoring by the defence in his early days with the Kings.
In 1974–75 his speed helped him set the league record
for most short-handed goals in a single season, with 10.

Goaltender Rogie Vachon was the first star for the Kings—classic mask!

The Forum, impressive home of the Los Angeles Kings.

Marcel with two L.A. success stories—Jack Kent Cooke (top)
and Glenn Frey of the Eagles (bottom).

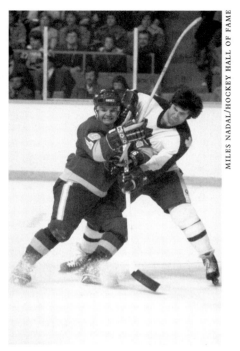

Ian Turnbull is moved by
Dionne's incredible strength.

Battling the Czechs
for Team Canada.

Team Canada 1976 (left to right: Serge Savard, Marcel Dionne,
Lanny McDonald, Gilbert Perreault and Bobby Hull).

Triple Crown Line sniper
Charlie Simmer.

Dionne and defensive-zone
responsibility Wayne Gretzky.

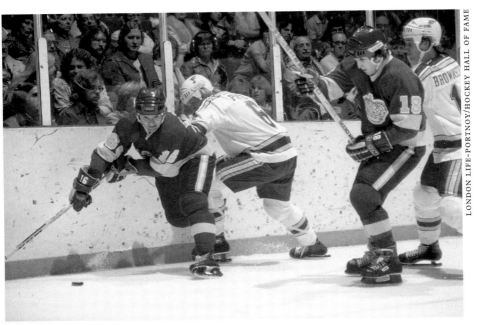

Two thirds of the Triple Crown—Dave Taylor clears the passing lane for Dionne.

Veteran Dionne sporting a Rangers jersey.
In the 1987–88 season Marcel would prove his worth
by scoring 22 of his 31 goals for New York on the power play.

The Dionne family at Gilbert Jr.'s wedding (left to right: Chantal, Lorraine,
Rénald, Gilbert Jr., Laurette, Gilbert Sr., Marlène, Marcel, Linda and Guylaine).

Carol and Marcel with their children at his 1992 induction to the Hockey Hall of Fame (left to right: Marcel, Garrett, Carol, Drew and Lisa).

Laurette and Gilbert Sr., on their 50th wedding anniversary.

Gilbert Jr. (left) confers with Mike Keane during the Stanley Cup playoffs.

The Dionne brothers and their wives celebrate winning
the Stanley Cup with the Montreal Canadiens in 1993
(left to right: Carol, Gilbert's wife, Heather, Gilbert Jr. and Marcel).

found that if I prepared myself, and Davey and Marcel were the same, the distractions were fun. If you just focused on your job, it was an easy place to play."

Talented players, such as those on the Triple Crown Line, could see a future in hockey and understood the benefit of remaining focused. For those whose talents in hockey allowed them to live in the moment, their place on the L.A. social scene was here today and perhaps gone tomorrow. Thus, not a moment was to be wasted. And so, while Marcel Dionne can reflect on a career of great accomplishments that earned him a spot in the Hall of Fame, other members of the Los Angeles Kings are left to savour their own measures of success.

Glenn Goldup was one of those for whom success didn't always result from hockey. "I was living with a Playmate at the time: Lorraine Michaels. She was Miss April 1980, I think. I had met this girl, and she wanted to try out for *Playboy* magazine and she made it. So I ended up getting on all the party lists and went to all the Midsummer Night's Dream parties and the Friday movie nights. I broke that ground; that was my baby. And Charlie Simmer and I were living together, so Lorraine and I introduced him to the Playmate of the Year that year and he ended up marrying her.

"But I'm the *only* one from that team that's been in the magazine," Goldup stresses. "And you know what? I was player of the week in the NHL one week, and nobody called or said anything. But when *Playboy* magazine came out and my picture was in it, I got calls from Vancouver to New York—all of my buddies everywhere!

"So, we'd just go up to the Playboy mansion and spend the day. They would have a buffet out and there'd be all kinds of famous people there. Bill Cosby was there, Magic Johnson was often there. I mean, you name it, they were all there."

Not only was it a privilege to be in such exclusive company, but the opportunity to partake of the actual goings-on at the home of Hugh Hefner was a thrill on its own. Of all the subtleties to be absorbed, what Goldup found astonishing was the innkeeper's omnipresent eye. "One night after a Midsummer Night's Dream party, where you would party all night and go to bed at five o'clock in the morning and get up at one or two the next afternoon, we went into the breakfast room and sat down. I slept in the guest house with my girlfriend. So, the night before I'm at the party and I'm drinking beer. And I'm drinking it out of the can. I asked the guy for a Budweiser and told him to just bring it in the can. Sometime during the night, after my first one, a guy walks over and he says, 'Excuse me, Mr. Goldup, but Mr. Hefner prefers that you use the crystal at his parties.' I go, 'No problem.' I mean, give me the crystal; pour it in, that's it.

"So, this next afternoon we woke up and went to breakfast. There were five or six Playmates, a couple of other guys who stayed over, Lorraine and myself. I order a beer. Now, up to that point I had never met Mr. Hefner. Well, honest to God, I don't know how this happened or came about, but the guy returns with the beer and says, 'Mr. Hefner says you can drink out of a can today.'

"Hugh came in about ten minutes later and introduced himself. He sat down at the table and we chatted. He was very fatherly to the girls—he took care of them and he was a very well-spoken man. I mean, the guy wasn't nuts; he was very intelligent. He was portrayed to be a womanizer, which he was to the max, but everything else about him was very classy. Actually, quite a nice person to sit down and have a conversation with."

While it is quite likely that the chief regret of every non-winning NHLer is to have never tasted champagne from the Stanley Cup, a few L.A. Kings might say that drinking Budweiser from the crystal at the Playboy mansion is a small consolation. Small indeed.

Chapter Ten

A S THE KINGS began the 1980–81 season, fans and players alike anticipated more of the same from the Triple Crown Line. As the season got rolling, so did the combination of Simmer, Dionne and Taylor. Although Edmonton's Wayne Gretzky would win the scoring crown with an amazing total of 164 points, a new league record, Marcel had another outstanding year, leading the Kings with 135 points, followed by Taylor with 112 and Simmer with 105.

The continued success of this high-profile unit made it easy for owner Jerry Buss to embrace the team. And despite his unconventional image as an NHL club owner, he wanted the best for the Kings and tried to learn all he could about the game of hockey. Rogie Vachon, who would become general manager of the Kings in the 1983–84 season, was amazed by the genuine interest his boss took in understanding the finer points of the game. "I loved working for Dr. Buss. He's a pretty neat guy. He wanted to learn so much about hockey. Originally, when he bought the team, he didn't know a lot about hockey. He knew a lot about basketball, and obviously had a very successful career as owner of the L.A. Lakers.

"After every game, he would come into my office, and sometimes he would come in with a little girlfriend and would send her home with a driver. But he would spend all night—*all* night, until eight or nine in the morning—in my office. And we'd just talk— talk about hockey and strategy. It was just unbelievable. He did that many nights."

Buss's willingness to secure the players that would better his team led to noticeable improvements on the Kings roster. Two of the more significant additions came with the arrivals of future

Hall of Fame defenceman Larry Murphy, and former Buffalo Sabre Jerry Korab (acquired in the latter portion of the 1979–80 season). In his rookie season, 1980–81, Murphy scored 76 points, good for fourth on the Kings—an impressive showing. Korab also proved to be a solid acquisition for the blue line. However, management's decision to take a risk on another Buffalo Sabre, Richard Martin, didn't pan out as well.

A badly damaged knee meant that Martin's days on the ice were numbered. By March 1981 he had played in only 23 games, and Buffalo wisely decided to trade him. Not as shrewd as the Sabres' management, the Kings gave up two valuable draft picks to see Martin play in one game that season and only three in the next before he was forced to call it a career.

Back when recovery remained a possibility, Martin was treated to the hospitality of Jerry Buss and the company of assorted Hollywood stars. If nothing else, he was entertained during his brief stint out west. At one home game, Martin hung out with the popular television star Hervé Villechaize, better known as "Tattoo" on the series *Fantasy Island*. "Rick wasn't playing, because his knee was wrecked, but he stayed with us the entire year," says Dionne. "He'd meet all the stars with Jerry Buss because they came to the games. So, this one evening he brings Hervé Villechaize into the dressing room. It was kind of funny because here was this little guy walking around with Rick. And Rick asked him, 'How do you protect yourself?'" Dionne imitates the actor's distinctive voice to offer the response. "'Hey, Rrrick. I don't worry about the big guys,' he says. 'Look!' And he shows everyone this little gun that he had tucked inside his cowboy boot. Poor Hervé wants to meet all the players, but it's after the game and all these big naked guys are coming out of the shower . . . Jerry Korab—six foot three, and his *thing* almost hit Hervé in the face! So, after that evening they called me Tattoo. 'Hey, Tattoo, da plane, da plane!'"

The end of the 1980–81 season was once again marked by a quick exit from the playoffs. Prior to the commencement of the following year's schedule, the international game would once again take the spotlight. Canada had won in dramatic fashion in 1972 and convincingly in 1976. But the 1981 Canada Cup would be the first time Canada tasted defeat while competing with a team made up of its best.

While Marcel Dionne dutifully answered the call to play for Canada, he felt he had to prove himself to earn his place on the team despite his consistency in NHL regular-season play. Given Canada's stockpile of talent, his concern was understandable.

"It always came back to survival for me," Marcel says. "It was never automatic that I would play. It wasn't in '76, nor was it in '81; for other players, yes, it *was* automatic. For example, in 1981 they sat me out a game. I was a bit of a slow starter and I wasn't happy with my first game myself, but that's the way it goes. I remember that Red Berenson, who was the assistant coach, stuck by me and told them, 'Hey, don't worry about Marcel, he'll be there.'

"What happened in '81 was that Gilbert Perreault broke his ankle. And they had sat me out a game and put Kenny Linseman in instead of me. Those are the numbers, and you don't make a big thing of it. But I was at the game, and was happy to be there with my wife, and you understand the concept of that type of series, you're part of the team. But the press makes such a big thing of it. So the next morning you pick up the paper and have a coffee and you read, 'That's going to get Dionne going!' What do you mean, it's gonna get me going? It's just the way it is and I was happy for Kenny to play.

"Then we had a practice, and suddenly there were twenty writers wanting to talk to me because I was taking Gilbert Perreault's place. I felt bad that I got into the lineup because of his injury, and I was devastated for Gilbert because we were roommates at training camp and he was playing so well. So, we're practising and I'm trying to get back to work and I didn't want to talk to the press. I said, 'That's it, I'm just here to play.'"

When Dionne replaced Perreault, he landed on a line with Wayne Gretzky and Guy Lafleur. However, what should have been a brilliant unit stalled, as the trio were unable to make the necessary adjustments to each other's dominating styles.

Marcel recalls the difficulties: "Looking back, it was a tough situation because Wayne's style was similar to my own. What you need to do with Wayne is just give it to him and get in the hole. I mean, he was *the* playmaker. But when you have the ability to do things, you hold onto the puck, you beat a guy. It's difficult to do less than what you are capable of. If I were to go back and play with Wayne, I would have focused a little more on just giving it to him and using less of my ability. Let him be the guy. Remember, Lafleur was an up-and-down guy. He would just get in the open and get that shot—*boom!* That was Flower's style. So, in '81, it was a different role for me. Although I experienced that with Bobby Hull and Phil Esposito in '76, where I was just feeding them, being their guy, I didn't have the time to really focus on that with Wayne and I think that was the difference. You've got to step back. He's the guy, he's gonna make you. Even if you think, 'Yeah, I can do this'—no. Give it to him and he'll find you. But we didn't have the time. I only played a couple of games with him and it was done."

Although Marcel contributed a respectable four goals and one assist over the course of the tournament, all of Team Canada came up flat in the one-game final against the Soviet Union. Canada had thumped the Soviets 7–3 during the round robin, but the goaltending of the great Vladislav Tretiak (who was named the tournament MVP) was the major difference in the final. The score of the championship game was 8–1. It remains somewhat of a low point in the history of Team Canada performances.

Back in Los Angeles, Dionne decided to try a new approach towards dealing with the press. Each year, he had been the focus of their attention, and he simply wanted to take a break. Up until that point, as teammate Mike Murphy attests, Dionne had shouldered the burden as cooperatively as possible. "Marcel was a very quotable player and a very visible player amongst the media in L.A. because he performed so well on the ice and scored so much. So he became the focal point for the media, which was correct. And Marcel was an accountable, standup guy. When there were problems, or when they wanted a game story, or a line on the game, Marcel would sit down and do his business, which is the job of all players, to be accountable to the media. And I think Marcel was excellent in that area. He stood there and took his medicine when it didn't go well and made comments when it did go well. He wasn't a fair-weather child. He didn't run away when things were going tough or bad."

Having to deal with an exhaustive barrage of media day in and day out undoubtedly took a toll. And so, Marcel returned from the Canada Cup and respectfully stood his ground with the press. "I told them I was tired of answering questions about our team, about living in Hollywood, that we're not good enough, that I'm a selfish guy. I'm just so tired of everything. You know what? I just want to play. Let's see what happens. And the press got pissed off. They hate you for that, but they don't understand. It was probably the most enjoyable year of hockey in my career. I knew that whatever was said in the newspapers, it didn't come from me. I really enjoyed that."

Aside from the freedom afforded by his personal boycott of the press, 1981–82 would turn out to be truly memorable for a most satisfying reason. At the conclusion of the regular-season schedule the Kings were to go on to enjoy an extraordinary playoff series against the Edmonton Oilers. However, the road to the playoffs did have a few bumps along the way.

The team began the season with yet another new head coach, Parker MacDonald, who would be replaced by Don Perry near the halfway point. The confidence and sense of stability gained under Bob Berry took a substantial hit. To make matters worse, after two very productive seasons, the Triple Crown Line sustained a crushing blow.

Bob Miller remembers: "In Toronto, Charlie Simmer broke his leg, and it was a really bad break. We didn't know on our telecast how serious it was, but Charlie broke it along the boards and they had brought the stretcher out. I remember we had a shot of Marcel, who skated over, looked at Charlie on the ice, went over to the bench, put his head down and shook his head back and forth. Right away I knew this was a serious injury. Marcel just shook his head like he was in despair, because at that time they were at the height of their popularity and effectiveness, and he knew if Charlie ever played again, it was going to take a long time."

Once again, the NHL's lead story that season was Wayne Gretzky, who went on a goal-scoring spree that established a record that stands to this day. The Great One scored a phenomenal 92 goals, shattering Phil Esposito's mark of 76. He racked up his first 50 goals in just 39 games, besting the standard of "50 in 50," established by Rocket Richard and equalled by Mike Bossy. Having finished the schedule second only to the New York Islanders, Gretzky's Edmonton Oilers couldn't help but feel confident heading into their first-round playoff series against the Kings, who ended their season with 63 points to the Oilers' 111.

After Simmer's injury caused him to miss 30 games, he was able to return in time to help his team prepare for the playoffs. Simmer recalls that L.A. played with an intensity that was a direct response to the cockiness of a team that was on the cusp of becoming hockey's next dynasty. "It was an up-and-down year that year. I was just coming back from a broken leg, and I think Edmonton had 48 more points than we did in the standings. We just made it [into the playoffs] because we had a better record than Colorado [who finished the year with a paltry 49 points]. But I think there was a lot of motivation for our team, not only amongst the players themselves, but because of some of the players on Edmonton.

"They had every right to be ridiculing us and laughing at us, because they finished so far ahead of us in the standings and they had so much talent. Yet I think by winning the first game up there, a real close battle, 10–8, our confidence started to build and you could start to see the possibility that we could actually beat them. That was very fulfilling, that an underdog that big could do it. And they had done it the year before, to Montreal."

While giving up eight goals was hardly cause for celebration, it did show that the Kings could play Edmonton's game and survive. How long they could do so remained to be seen, as Edmonton won the next game 3–2 before the series shifted to L.A. What followed was the greatest comeback in NHL playoff history, a feat that lives in hockey lore as "The Miracle on Manchester." Bob Miller called the play-by-play. "We got into that best-of-five series with Edmonton, and of course nobody thought we had a chance at all. The first game up there ended up 10–8, which was the most playoff goals scored by two teams in one game. Then, the next game in Edmonton, the Oilers won. So we came back to Los Angeles with the series tied, and everybody is excited because the Kings won game one. The Forum is sold out; there was a lot of publicity in Los Angeles for the game. At the end of two periods, we're losing 5–0.

"I was upset. You know, the history of the team to that point had been that every time we get the city excited about the Kings and hockey, we go right into the dumper. We just go right down the tubes. So here it is, 5–0 for the Oilers at the end of two, and I just thought, here we've done it again. We got everybody excited and now we're just blowing it.

"So now we come out and Jay Wells scores early in the third period. I remember thinking, well, at least it wasn't a shutout. And then Doug Smith scores, and it's 5–2. Charlie Simmer scored next, and at that point you could just sense it in the Forum—the fans thinking, 'It's 5–3, maybe there's a chance.' All of a sudden, throughout the whole building, you could just feel the energy.

"Prior to this, the Oilers were an arrogant, arrogant team. You know all of those young guys—Gretzky, Messier and Glenn Anderson. They were on the bench, laughing at the Kings' power play. Somebody on the Kings bench said, 'Hey, they're laughing at us over there.' They were just downright arrogant. And [coach] Glen Sather had that smirk on his face behind the bench.

"So now the Kings fans are on their feet and the place is starting to go crazy. Then there are two breakaways by Pat Hughes of Edmonton. He shoots over the net on one, and Mario Lessard, the Kings' goalie, stops him twice on the other. First the shot and again on the rebound. With 4:01 left in the third, Mark Hardy scores for the Kings, it's 5–4 and the place is bedlam, absolute bedlam. They go down to about the final ten seconds, and Wayne Gretzky gets the puck for Edmonton, in the Edmonton zone. If he clears it, the game is over. Jimmy Fox of the Kings steps in front of Gretzky and takes the puck away from him, centres it up the middle to the top of the slot to Mark Hardy. Hardy shoots. Grant Fuhr makes the save, and the rebound comes to another Kings rookie, Steve Bozek, and he scores. My voice was cracking and I'm screaming, 'Bozek scores!' And I look at the clock and there's five seconds left.

"I remember Grant Fuhr's reaction. He had that plain white mask that they used to wear in those days, and he put his head down, and it was like you could almost see through the mask to see the disappointment on his face. That's how graphic his disappointment was.

"Then we get into overtime, and early on the Oilers have a great chance to win it. Lessard slides out of the net to stop the puck and doesn't get it. Messier picks up the puck, and the net is wide open and he shoots on the backhand—high and wide to the right.

"At 2:35 of the overtime, the face-off is in the Oilers zone and the Kings have three rookies up front: Smith, Bozek and Evans. Bozek wins the draw back to Daryl Evans, and he fires it into the net from the right circle, right over the shoulder of Grant Fuhr. They said they were leaving the parking lot with Oilers jerseys tied to their bumpers.

"As far as individual games go, no one will ever forget this one. But in fact, Jerry Buss, the Kings' owner, had left. I remember looking down where he used to sit in a little box of his own, right between the two benches, right at the glass. I looked down early in the third period and it was empty, and I thought, 'Geez, has he left the game?' Well, I found out that he was headed to Palm Springs, and he figured, 5–0, I'm gone. They had the game on the radio in the limousine and I understand that the chauffeur, when it got to be 5–3, said, 'Should we go back?' And reportedly, Buss said, 'No, the farther we get away, the better they seem to do.' So he kept going and the owner missed the greatest individual game in Kings history."

From the point of view of the Kings players, when they fell behind 5–0 heading into the third period they wanted simply to save face. Charlie Simmer recalls the mood in the dressing room during the second intermission. "In between periods, we just talked about, 'Let's not be embarrassed. Let's not give them any more and we'll just go one at a time.' And they'd be skating by our bench, you know, 'We'll see you later, boys, you guys are done.' Dave Lumley was one of their guys that was pretty adamant about yakking back. Guys like Wayne, Mark and Jari Kurri would never embarrass you. It was more the [peripheral] players. But then we got one, two, and all of a sudden it was 5–3. It just started to escalate as the period went on. Of course, they had great chances to score, but Lady Luck was on our side."

After "The Miracle on Manchester," the Oilers rallied in game four, again winning 3–2, to force a fifth and deciding game the next day. The two teams ended up sharing a late-night charter to Edmonton, an arrangement Jerry Buss agreed to with the proviso that his team sit at the front of the plane. That way, the Kings could exit the plane before the Oilers, and it was guaranteed that any holdups at customs would hamper both teams' chances of salvaging a night's rest.

Running on adrenaline with little sleep, the Los Angeles Kings were to shock everyone with their performance in the fifth game.

The pundits saw little on the L.A. roster, beyond the Triple Crown Line, to convince them the Kings could challenge the young and bucking Oilers. Indeed, most of the Kings were either rookies or players with little playoff experience. Dionne's composed leadership would prove to be the factor that tilted the scales in the Kings' favour.

"Marcel was just outstanding that night," Mike Murphy says. "He led the way, not just scoring-wise, but he led the way emotionally and mentally. He just had great poise, was under control emotionally, under control physically. He played like a real superstar that night. And he played that way the entire series, but that night in particular comes to mind."

With their decisive 7–4 victory in the deciding game, Dionne and his teammates delivered the first real taste of hockey success to Los Angeles. To that date, the win over the Oilers was the high point in the franchise's relatively short history. On a more personal level for Dionne, his role in defeating an overly confident Oilers team garnered a degree of respect that had long eluded both him and the Kings. And perhaps most important of all, in an unspoken fashion, Dionne had proved that his dedication to excellence was not wasted in L.A.

In the second round of the playoffs, the Kings met the Vancouver Canucks. Although the first four games of their best-of-seven series were decided by a one-goal margin, the Kings ultimately lost in five. On the strength of their goaltender, Richard Brodeur, the Canucks made it to the Stanley Cup finals, where they were beaten soundly by the New York Islanders.

While many players might have been satisfied to have been part of an upset on the magnitude of L.A.'s defeat of Edmonton, Marcel's voracious appetite for competition left him craving another challenge. For this reason, when the opportunity arose to play in the postseason World Championships, he agreed happily to play for his country. "It was extremely important to me, playing in the World Championships. To play amongst the best players in the world, I needed that, to perform at a higher level. In a lot of ways, the World Championships were my salvation."

Far from a consolation prize for missing—or making an early exit from—the NHL playoffs, Dionne insists that the Worlds are a learning opportunity that is not to be dismissed lightly. "As the years go by, it's getting tougher and tougher for the teams in the World Championships to get NHL players. A lot of guys decline [the invitation]. Granted, the financial aspect is a big concern, but we were made as hockey players, and to compete is the ultimate. That's what we're supposed to do, go into the unknown and try to better ourselves. Guys who find excuses [not to play], they're not the real deal. Hockey is about more than winning. And it's more than money, or even the commitment to play in the NHL. It's about experiences and feeling everything the game has to offer. You have the chance to play with other players, in other countries where hockey is huge—that's what it's all about. It's a universal sport. If guys don't want to experience that, they're missing something."

After the next season, 1982–83, Marcel's wife Carol was expecting their second of two boys—Garrett had been the first, and Drew was about to arrive. Despite Dionne's fifth consecutive 50-goal campaign, the team missed the playoffs completely. This freed Marcel to help out on the domestic front. When the call came from Alan Eagleson to play for Canada in the World Championships this time, he had good reason to take a pass.

"Drew was two days old and I really didn't feel like going," Marcel says. "I couldn't believe anybody would call. I said forget it."

"[Eagleson] begged Marcel," Carol remembers. "Marcel said, 'No. My wife just had a baby and I have to stay at home.' But I told him that he should go. I said, 'This might be your last one. And what would you do at home? Follow me around the house?'"

"So then I went, and believe it or not, I was gone for a whole month!" Marcel chimes in. "I was with Charlie Simmer and Dave

Taylor. For the first eight days, we met Team Canada and played exhibition games. We were the only pros playing with all of these young guys—James Patrick, Pat Flatley, they were both playing then. Well, it was probably one of the best experiences I ever had, playing with these kids aspiring to make the NHL. We did pretty well in those exhibition games, and then the NHL players arrived and replaced them."

Memories of that time have also stuck with Charlie Simmer as being most enjoyable. The Triple Crown Line was given the chance to showcase its talent for the European hockey community while learning a fresh approach to the game under coach Dave King.

"Actually, we had a better year with Los Angeles than we had the year before," Simmer shrugs, "but we didn't make the playoffs. So we were able to go over there a week or so early because they needed players. We ended up going to Prague, Germany, back up to Sweden, and then returned to Germany where the tournament was. We had a great time.

"Dave King was the head coach. I always liked him. It was a little different for us because of the different coaching style. He had all kinds of sayings for what he wanted us to do—'come up the back door,' or 'the quiet zone.' It was more or less the way that hockey was going, but we hadn't experienced it yet with L.A. So it was an exciting time.

"We were having a lot of fun with it, and then more of the NHL players started to come and it got a little political. I know at one time they wanted to send me home because they said my skating wasn't strong enough. And Marce stuck up for me. He said, 'No, we've come all the way over here together, we're going to play together.' But they brought over some different players. I know Bob Gainey and I sort of platooned off the wing with those two guys [Taylor and Dionne], but when it came down to it, we scored some big goals together. And I think that really helped out. It was fun sticking together like that."

While Simmer was grateful for Dionne's support, Marcel laments that a stronger case should have been made on his linemate's behalf. "When we arrived, Dave King was really in control. And when it was just the three of us, we fit right in. This was before the rest of the pros showed up, so King was not intimidated. But when the other guys came, and he was dealing strictly with pros, I could see he didn't respond the same way. I was playing with Charlie and Dave and we should have stuck together. But he didn't feel the speed was there. So I was playing with Bob Gainey. And Bob is a great guy to play with, but frick, he couldn't put the puck in the ocean. Great two-way player, but in that type of series, you need to score goals, too."

Because the format and timing of the World Championships prevented Canada from putting its very best players on the ice (they took place during the NHL playoffs), the national side consistently finished with modest results. Nevertheless, the competition and bonding amongst the players served them well. As it turned out, the 1983 World Championships would not be Dionne's last. In 1986, he would return to Moscow to play for Canada once more. On that occasion, the coach was the man who would soon take over behind the bench in Los Angeles: Pat Quinn.

Having failed for several years to do much in the playoffs, and having missed them completely in 1983, the Los Angeles Kings had to get their house in order. Not surprisingly, their 1983–84 season would be marked by frustration, multiple coaching changes, and the failure to make the playoffs for the second year in a row.

Although the team's results were poor, the outlook wasn't devoid of positives. Along with the old faithful Triple Crown Line, the Kings' new scoring sensation, Bernie Nicholls, confirmed his potential by leading the team in points (41 goals, 54 assists, for 95 points). Charlie Simmer recalls one way in which the rookie benefited from Dionne's direction. "When Bernie first got there he was a raw and cocky kid. He had a great shot and was a very good offensive player. I remember one game—Bernie was put out on the power play with us and he was going all over the place. Finally, Marcel looked at him and said, 'Bernie, go stand over there, and don't move!' Sure enough, he scored three power play goals that game. It was hilarious. It was like, 'Bernie, just go there and be quiet.' Everybody would be concentrating on Marcel and Bernie would just be standing there, like he's a rookie, he's not very good. Marce would slide over a one-timer and it would be in the net."

Keeping pace with Nicholls, both Simmer, who avoided injury for the second year running, and Dionne, who played 66 games, finished with 92 points (Simmer with 44 goals, 48 assists; Dionne, 39 goals, 53 assists). But, inevitably, all that was could not remain. In the summer of '84, coming off his best season in three years, Charlie entered contract talks with management. Having attained the status of an accomplished NHL goal scorer, the Triple Crown sniper wanted to be compensated as such. During this process he sought Dionne's counsel. "Marce was good. We all wanted to stick together, but he said, 'At this point, it's a business. You've got to do what's right for you. You're not here for a long time, so you definitely need to earn what you think you deserve—and then you go from there.'"

Simmer played five games for the Kings at the start of the 1984–85 season before he was traded to the Boston Bruins for a first-round draft pick. "I look at that now, which is easy to do, and I think something could have been worked out and we could have stayed together a lot longer, which I would have really liked," assesses Simmer with some regret. "Because the Triple Crown Line was, of course, a line that made me. But it also made me realize the confidence I had in my game, that I could make it."

With the departure of one of the most popular Kings, it appeared as if serious plans for the future were being put into motion. Still, Dionne had plenty of gas in his tank and remained the on-ice leader of the Kings. All he could do was await the improvements that he thought might follow the arrival of coach Pat Quinn.

Chapter Eleven

B Y 1984, the Edmonton Oilers had met their destiny and won their first Stanley Cup in what would become a run of five in seven years. It was therefore virtually mandatory that the rest of the league retool and devise strategies based on beating the Edmonton powerhouse. In the case of the aging Montreal Canadiens, a new style of play introduced by coach Jacques Lemaire indicated that the era of the Habs' legendary brand of "firewagon" hockey was over. The ramifications for the freewheeling Guy Lafleur, and his linemate Steve Shutt, were painfully clear.

"It was getting near the end of the line," remembers Shutt. "I guess I was thirty-two and Jacques Lemaire had come in as coach and decided that, looking at the talent on our team, we were going to play the trap. And I mean, I can't play the trap; Lafleur can't play the trap. As a result, our ice time just went right down.

"So I didn't play that much, and then we got into the playoffs and I was in and out of the lineup—in one game, out another game—and I was never on a regular line, but I was leading our team in scoring, so it was a little frustrating [Shutt had 7 goals in the '84 playoffs, more than any other Hab]. We were going to play that trap system right to the end."

Shutt was not ready to be put out to pasture just yet. As veterans do, he could envision himself in the role of helping a team bring along its younger talent. Having spoken to Mike Murphy, who was then the assistant coach under Pat Quinn in L.A., Shutt had his assignment all lined up. "So we go into the next year, Lemaire is still there, and Lafleur, you know, he wants to get traded, so I go up to see Serge [Savard, the general manager]. I said, 'Serge, this is not going to work.' He said, 'Okay, here are your options. You stay here and be in and out of the lineup, you can go down and be a playing assistant coach to Pat Burns in Sherbrooke, or we can trade you.' And I said, 'Well, I've already talked with L.A. and they would like to get me.' He said, 'Okay, fine, we'll work out a deal.' I said, 'There's only one problem. I've got three years left on my contract and they don't want to pick up all three years.' And he said, 'Fine. You go there and play as long as you want, then after that, we'll pick you up and look after whatever is left on your contract.' Serge was great. And that's exactly how we left it. So I got traded for a seventh-round pick, or whatever it was, and when I was finished there, the Canadiens picked me up on waivers for a hundred bucks. But that's the way the organization has always been; the Montreal Canadiens have always been a first-class organization."

Coming from the winningest franchise in hockey history, and having played a key role in their recent success, Shutt was in for a surprise. Among other things, playing his final season in Los Angeles impressed upon him just how difficult the conditions were that Marcel Dionne played under. Going from a perpetual Stanley Cup contender to a team that struggled to keep the score close in a regular-season game was a rude awakening for the Hall of Famer.

"The difference was, in Montreal, we knew that if everybody played up to their capabilities, we're going to win the game. It was as simple as that. There was no question about it. We had that confidence. We were going to win every single game; that's what was in our minds.

"When you got out to Los Angeles, where you could play your best possible game and it still wasn't good enough, it was like, 'Wow, wait a minute. I'm not used to *this*.' And Marcel didn't have very good teams to play with in Detroit, nor in his first couple of years in L.A. So you have to have a totally different mindset. You can't worry about what the score is, you just have to go out and play your best. It doesn't matter whether the score it is 2–2 or 8–2, you can't let the score get in the way.

"In Montreal, we could focus more on the score because we'd

be in the games, every single game. Whereas, on some of the teams Marcel played for—I mean, after the first period, the game was over. He couldn't just say, 'Well, geez, the game's over, I'm not going to play.' He had to refocus and say, 'I don't care what the score is, I'm going to play the best I can.' It's probably tougher to play how Marcel did than how we did in Montreal because it gets discouraging."

Shutt also noticed a decidedly lackadaisical attitude that was symptomatic of that period in Los Angeles. A standard of professionalism, on and off the ice, was sorely needed. To get the young talent to buy into that program was the challenge that Shutt faced. It was the same task that Dionne had struggled with for years.

"When I went out to Los Angeles, I don't think the younger guys were as focused as they could have been," Shutt submits. "And Marcel would get frustrated. He would stand up and say his piece, but some of the guys were sitting there going, 'Yeah, it's Marcel. Look at him talking, he's playing thirty minutes a game,' and a lot of them would slough it off.

"But when Marcel came to the rink, he was focused for every game—ready to play. And that's what a leader is all about. Whether it's the Montreal Forum or the L.A. Forum, the temperature inside the building is the same. But don't forget, this was a different era. When you went from the 1960s and '70s to the 1980s and '90s, you just couldn't tell the players what to do anymore.

"I'll give you a classic story, just a beautiful story about Serge Savard. Serge was playing junior back when Scotty [Bowman] was the coach and Sam [Pollock] was the general manager. When they used to go on the road, the lights and TVs had to be off at ten o'clock at night. That was the team rule. So Scotty would go with a passkey, open the door to a room, and run in and check if the TV was still hot. This way he would know if the guy had just turned the TV off.

"So he was doing his rounds like this, opens the door to Serge's room, runs over, goes to check if the TV is still hot, and Savard has got it wrapped in a towel with ice sitting on top of it. Scotty looks at him, and Serge says, 'Scotty, I just pulled my groin!' So there were little games like this because of the control they had over the players in the '60s. But stuff like that, you wouldn't have to do in the '90s.

"In Los Angeles, I think what happened was that there were a couple of players there who they were trying to groom. These guys were going to be the leaders of the future. But a lot of these guys didn't want to be the leaders; they just wanted to go and play and that was it. But as you know, as you get older, you've got to take over the leadership role. So at times they ridiculed Marcel for being a leader—you know, they thought it was funny. Sure, real funny. And it was tough on Marcel.

"I would go and grab some of the guys. I would do it one on one with the guy and say, 'Lookit, you're going to be one of the leaders here. You're one of the guys that is going to have to be responsible.' I'd put it right in front of the guy. I would do it privately, go out for a beer with the guy.

"The one thing I learned from Montreal was that leadership starts on the ice. You can talk all you want, but do it on the ice. I mean, Henri Richard never said boo. Guy Lafleur never said boo. They did it on the ice. Jean Béliveau was never a big 'rah-rah-rah' guy. You can say all you want, but if you don't do it on the ice, it means nothing."

The most gifted of the younger Kings—on the ice, at least—was Bernie Nicholls. After leading the team in scoring in 1983–84, Nicholls bettered his production in '84–85 by reaching the 100-point plateau (46 goals, 54 assists), second only to Dionne, who had his best output in four years with 126 points (46 goals, 80 assists). But while Nicholls had the requisite skill with the puck, it appeared that he could be less than enthused about serious matters off the ice.

Whether it was Dionne's enviable position as a franchise player, or simply that he was too driven for the likes of some, his leadership elicited an uneven response from the other Kings. And Nicholls was one player who seemed noticeably put off by Dionne. "Bernie is a guy that had tremendous ability," Marcel reflects. "But I always felt he could have given a lot more as far as leadership goes on the team. With his ability to play, he could do it. Bernie was just different, and I had a tough time—he gave me a tough time. Maybe I was too much, and I know that I was too much. When I left L.A., I discovered that you can't be everything at all times.

"But Bernie had a great shot. And I always thought he could be a leader. You know, get up in that dressing room and say something serious. Instead, he just went along with things. But to just go along like that wasn't good enough. He wanted to be *the* guy, which is fine. But to be *the* guy, you've got to stand up and say something, at least sometimes. You can't *just* have fun. This thing is a business."

Charlie Simmer adds: "That's what would bother Marcel. Bernie was the type of player that was very relaxed. He was a cowboy, really. Nothing much bothered him—winning *or* losing. I think the care and love of the game—not that Bernie didn't have it, he had it in his own way, but that would upset Marcel, who was very intense at all times. So you're looking at a very relaxed guy— a cowboy, if you want to call him that—from Haliburton [Ontario], and then Marcel with his intensity. I mean, definitely oil and water."

Rightly or wrongly, Marcel Dionne always maintained that the Kings would benefit from a more serious approach; but the lack thereof seemed to be the one constant within the organization. Therefore, he was always on the lookout for dedicated players, especially those with an imposing physical presence, whom the Kings might be able to acquire. When Dave "Tiger" Williams was sent down to the Adirondack Red Wings of the AHL, Marcel made a probing call to his old Team Canada teammate, Darryl Sittler. With confirmation from Sittler that Tiger was in great shape, Dionne pitched the idea to management and, shortly thereafter, Williams became a Los Angeles King.

Dave Williams remembers, appreciatively, Dionne's role in bringing him to the Kings. "Marcel was the guy that got me to

L.A. He was a guy that paid attention to what was going on around the league. I was available and, actually, Marcel added three years onto my career. If it wasn't for Marcel taking the initiative to pick up the phone and call Sittler, and if it wasn't for Sittler putting in the word—it doesn't happen very often where a player will directly help you in your career, other than with what happens on the ice. But off the ice it's very rare. It happens between coaches, but from player to player, it doesn't happen very often. And that's why Sittler and I have been friends a long time, and that's why Dionne and I became friends. I really got to know Marcel, and took the time to get to know him in L.A."

In Dionne's words, "Tiger was all excited, all fired up." While such occurrences are rare for a player on his way out, Tiger's stint in Los Angeles marked a legitimate resurgence for the veteran winger. In the 1985–86 campaign, he netted 20 goals with 29 helpers for 49 points, his third-best total in a fourteen-year career. With the leadership and toughness he added to the Kings' roster, the offense was a pleasant bonus. "This guy might have been one of the best physically trained athletes in our time," Mike Murphy gushes. "He was just an exceptionally trained hockey player, and was mentally strong. He had very limited ability, but he knew what he had to do to survive in the league and he did it. He played hard, tough hockey every night and was a hard, tough guy. And he demanded a lot of himself and a lot of his teammates. Tiger was one of those guys who might punch one of your guys in the nose in your own locker room, but the moment you stepped on the ice, if anybody went near that guy, he'd punch *them* in the nose. He was an extremely positive team guy."

Although Steve Shutt was let go that year, with Tiger placing fourth in scoring behind Nicholls, Dionne and Taylor, L.A.'s offence was in decent shape. Of course, the Williams approach to grooming the younger players differed somewhat from Shutt's. And it wasn't long before Williams taught team prankster Bernie Nicholls a lesson in respect.

"Tiger had written a book. So he came in with a box of books, and they would sell them for him at the concession stands at the games," Marcel explains. "So, after practice Bernie came into the dressing room and saw this box of Tiger's books. While Tiger was staying out on the ice shooting pucks, which he always did, Bernie took the box of books and put one in each guy's stall—like it was a gift from Tiger. But the guys didn't know what Bernie had done. I got the book, and I'm thinking, 'That's really nice of Tiger.' So Tiger comes in and the guys are thanking him, 'That's nice, Tiger, thanks.'

"Well, he's fuming. He's hot! And right away, he knew it was Bernie. He said, 'Bernie, you're dead! You're dead meat!' And we're all laughing, because Tiger was discouraged over the book sales. So we all gave the books back, but I knew Tiger wouldn't forget.

"The next day, Bernie didn't think too much of it. He was laughing and giggling, which was how it was. The guys were always having fun. Well, I sat right by the door in the dressing room. It was a narrow dressing room at our practice facility, the Culver City rink. It was primitive, a real dump. I always remember breathing in the exhaust fumes from the Zamboni there. So Tiger comes in, and I'm the first one to see him. He walks in, and he's got his bow and arrow that he goes hunting with. You've got to imagine all the guys in this narrow dressing room facing one another. And Bernie is sitting at the far end of the room. Tiger's at the door and he says, 'Bernie, you c—ksucker, you're DEAD!' He just pulled back on that bow and everybody hit the floor. Everybody! *Fffooom!* Well, there was a heating duct sticking out from the wall, and the arrow went right through it. And Tiger knew what he was doing. It scared the hell out of all of us; everybody was in shock. Believe me, Bernie didn't think it was too funny at all. Then Tiger says, 'So, you want to screw around with me?' I thought it was something out of the movie *The Deer Hunter*. That was Tiger. Bernie never fooled around with him again."

During the off-season, a group of players would go to Palm Springs to relax and play golf over a few days as guests of the golf club. In keeping with his manner on the ice, Tiger Williams could play equally hard off the ice, be it on a golf course or elsewhere. And he would do so with little regard for what might be considered conduct appropriate to a given venue. Recalling one of their golf excursions, Dionne described Tiger in top form. "You had to watch Tiger, because he was crazy. We all got drinking one night, and we were drinking heavily. He'd be cooking hamburgers, and if you weren't paying attention, look out. He was just an animal. He'd have a spatula, flipping burgers, and he'd say, 'How do you like your burger—medium?' And he would take the spatula and stick it on your arm—*ahhh!* He'd burn you and then laugh and laugh.

"So, we had a lot of guys staying in condos at this resort, and I got up early the next morning after this night of drinking. I went by the pool and saw what I thought was a dead body. It was totally naked, and from where I was, I could see these dark splotches on it. Well, I guess that night Tiger was drinking amaretto, which is a sweet drink with a lot of sugar in it, and he passed out. Because Palm Springs is hot, you can sleep outside at night. In the summer it's very nice. So, he's lying there totally naked, and I guess he must have gone for a Jacuzzi. But when I got closer to him, the dark splotches came to life. I realized that it was a trail of ants running up to his face because of the sugar around his mouth from the amaretto. Well, I laughed so hard; I'd never seen anything like it. I mean, there were ants everywhere—it was ugly. And he didn't feel a thing. He was completely out of it. Every time I tell that story with Tiger, he gives me that look, and then he laughs. He was too much.

"That same time, we were playing golf. I remember coming down the eighteenth hole and on the ninth hole, which was right there, there was this big pond. I was with [Kings teammate] Phil Sykes and I walked up to my ball, looked ahead, and I saw Tiger with a kid. Well, he had this kid over his shoulder. Phil wasn't too far from me, and I said, 'Phil, Phil! Look, he's going to do it.' Phil replied, 'Do what?' I said, 'Look, he's going to throw that kid in the pond.' And this was a frickin' exclusive country club.

"Well, at the same time on the ninth hole, I see these people hit their balls, and later we find out that it was the president and the general manager of the club playing a round. Now, for us to be there, we had to play with a member of the club. So we got the pro to come out and play with us and be quiet about it, and everything was fine. You know, it was good public relations for the club, and we had a couple of members [in our party], but there were a lot more of us playing who weren't members.

"So, sure enough, Tiger grabs this kid and throws him in the pond. And you could hear the people looking on, saying, 'Hey, he threw that kid in the pond.' And the kid was swearing at Tiger. You could hear him screaming, 'You motherf—ker!' What happened was, during the day, this kid and another kid were following Tiger around the course in a golf cart. The kid was the son of one of the friends that was playing with us. He was there for the ride and wanted to meet the hockey players. But he started getting cocky with Tiger and using foul language. Well, that's all you needed to do with Tiger, so he was like, 'You rich little brat,' and he threw him in the pond.

"Now we're all in trouble. So, I straightened things out because I golfed there all the time. My friend at the club asked Tiger to write a letter of apology for the incident, and Tiger said, 'There's no way I'm going to apologize to these people.'" Dionne laughs. "So, the story was that Tiger didn't have to worry about it because he was never invited back."

Although there was a certain unpredictability to his methods, during the season Dave Williams was a dedicated team player. Naturally, when he witnessed teammates repeatedly scurrying to make a 1:30 tee time after practice, he was not impressed. Williams felt that the team's needs should have been the top priority. In hopes of addressing the level of individual commitment,

Tiger would speak out, only to be enlightened on the difference between playing in Toronto versus L.A. Marcel remembers: "Tiger stood up and said, 'We have to make a commitment here, guys.' But suddenly all of the players, even Dave Taylor, said that it should be the responsibility of each individual. Well, that was the problem. Some of these individuals couldn't do it on their own. They needed that direction, like, 'Hey, guys, we're going to make a commitment here.' And I warned Tiger; I said, 'They're going to shut you down. You'll be amazed.'

"That's what L.A. is all about. In Toronto, you wouldn't have to make that kind of appeal. Guys like Dan Maloney, Darryl Sittler and Lanny McDonald would all be behind you. In L.A., it got to be the opposite of that. I remember we got Dave Langevin, who had played for the New York Islanders, and he said, 'Well, it should be up to the individual.' I thought, 'Here's a guy that came from winning four Stanley Cups with the Islanders, and in New York that wouldn't have been acceptable. And now it's acceptable in L.A.? It's up to the individual?'"

Even with two reputable hockey men in Rogie Vachon and Pat Quinn heading up the Kings' brass, the team never achieved a killer instinct under the ownership of Jerry Buss. While Buss always gave the impression of wanting to learn about the game, he would never attain—or retain, as the case might have been—the combination of knowledge and personnel that could produce a winner. In a meeting in which Dionne tried to help his ill-equipped boss, Marcel left disconcerted after being afforded an unsolicited glimpse into the Kings owner's private life. "I had a meeting with Jerry Buss one time. I just wanted to know the direction that the team was going in. There were a lot of rumours about different players, and I just thought he was lost. He had no clue about hockey and he admitted it to everybody. And at that time all of management were jockeying for positions, and he was listening to everybody. So I had lunch with him and said that perhaps he should talk to a neutral party to help him assess his management and his team. I suggested he call Jim Gregory. And he did give Jim a call, but Jim couldn't do it because he had just taken a job with Central Scouting [a branch of the NHL's head office].

"But what amazed me during our conversation, which tells you what it was like having an owner like Jerry Buss, he said: 'You know, Marcel, I'll tell you something. I own the L.A. Kings, I own the Lakers, I own the Forum, I've got a big limousine that takes me wherever I want to go, and I've got the Pickford mansion. And you know what? Last night I was in one of the bedrooms and I had an eighteen-year-old girl there, and I made love to her. Then I went to the next bedroom, where I had another eighteen-year-old girl waiting for me—and I made love to her.' And I'm thinking, 'Holy shit, what's he getting at? We go from hockey to *this*?' And he said, 'But you know what? This morning I got up and I wasn't happy.' He told me all this stuff—he's got money, he's got everything and still he's not happy. So then he says, 'Do you know why I'm not happy?' I said, 'No, why?' He said, 'Because the Kings lost last night.' I got up and said, 'Mr. Buss, it was nice meeting with you today, it was a nice lunch, thank you very much.' I don't think I ever spoke with him again."

For the players who had been on winning teams and knew what it took to succeed in the NHL, the impression that Buss left verged on laughable. To put it mildly, he was a far cry from what most veterans were used to. "Buss used to come into the dressing room after the games. The only thing was, he'd never come on his own," Tiger Williams remembers. "He always had some bimbo with him or some movie guy. There was always an entourage, so you never got to know the guy. And it was a pretty bizarre situation. We had players on the team dating his daughter, and she worked in the building. I mean, stuff like that would never happen in the Montreal Canadiens organization or in Edmonton."

Much as it might seem that the atmosphere around the Kings organization was polluted by what Dionne would deem inappropriate behaviour, the Kings still managed a few right turns. By the

1986–87 season, Pat Quinn had made it to his third year as head coach and proved to be a much stronger presence than his recent predecessors. The Kings would also welcome three rookies to their roster that year in Jimmy Carson, Steve Duchesne and Luc Robitaille. Excited by the influx of quality talent, Dionne pondered how he might help the players who would be the future of hockey in L.A.

At training camp, the young left winger Luc Robitaille particularly impressed Marcel. "From the first day at camp, I liked him very much. He was my roommate, and boy did he want to play. I only played with him for one year, but with Luc it felt like we had played together for ten years. He had the commitment, he wanted to play, wanted to be successful, and he had a strong family background. It was like everything I saw in him, I saw in myself. So I wanted to do what I could to help him along."

"Coming into L.A., my dream was to make the NHL," Robitaille says. "My thinking was, if I'm going to make the team, I wanted to make things as easy as possible for myself. I was nervous coming to L.A. because it was such a big city. You know, I'd been in the United States, but only a few times. So I went through training camp with the Kings, and in those days we were pretty much on the road the entire time. We'd spend the first two weeks in Victoria, B.C., and after that we were on the road up until the last two pre-season games. For the last week and a half we'd be in L.A., and then the season would start.

"Marcel was my roommate throughout camp, and he was talking to me, asking me questions about what I wanted to do. I told him that I probably wanted to live in a boarding house—you know, just find a family to live with because I wanted to concentrate on hockey. And I was never thinking about Marcel's family. That never even crossed my mind.

"We came back to L.A., and I think that we stayed in a hotel for about a week, right by the Forum. And if you know that area in Inglewood, everybody was telling us not to go out at night because it wasn't too safe. So Steve Duchesne, Jimmy Carson and myself would just stay in our rooms every night. About four or five days before the season started, Marcel went to see Rogie Vachon, who was the general manager, and said, 'Are these kids going to make the team? If they are, I want to take care of them.' So Rogie said yes, and that's when Marcel talked to me. He said, 'Would you come and stay at my house?' Actually, I think he just said, 'You're coming and staying at my house'"—Luc grins—"and that was it. He also took care of Jimmy Carson, who stayed at the neighbours' house right next door, and he found another friend's place for Steve Duchesne, who stayed probably a mile or two away from where we were.

"For me, as a player, he made things so much easier because I didn't have to worry about anything. All I had to worry about was going to play the games. He helped me with everything from getting a new car to little things like opening a new bank account. I stayed at his house, so I didn't have to go through the ordeal of finding an apartment, and his wife Carol cooked my meals. So all of these things allowed me to focus on hockey. I had no headaches. For a young guy, it really made things easy. He made a big difference in my career."

The talent that Dionne had seen in Luc Robitaille blossomed through the course of his first season. Along with being the top scorer on the Kings (45 goals and 39 assists), Luc won the Calder Trophy. Thrilled to have a player with such enthusiasm and skill on the team, Dionne showed his support by taking a lesson from the new recruits. When he joined the rookies to practise their one-timers, Robitaille was surprised to learn that Dionne had never attempted the drill in his lengthy and prolific career. "When Jimmy Carson and I came in that year, it was the 1986–87 season, we were scoring most of our goals on the one-timer shot. Well, I'm sure Marcel had seen it before, but he had never played with guys that were so geared on the one-timer. I remember at one practice, he said, 'All right, I'm gonna practise it with you guys.' So we started practising it with him, and it was hysterical. He looked like a guy who had never played hockey, trying to take these shots. We thought it was so funny. With all the goals he scored, we couldn't believe that he couldn't even do a one-timer. But, of course, Marcel was a great passer. He wanted to be the guy setting up the one-timer."

Just as Marcel had enjoyed the company of Alex Delvecchio in his rookie season, now it was his turn to unknowingly be a source of inspiration and amusement. "Marcel was very funny in the way that he stretched," Robitaille continues, barely containing his laughter. "He was really old-time hockey in that way. When I came into the league, the game was changing a little bit—you know, workout wise. And guys were really starting to stretch. I remember being in the locker room before games, and a lot of the guys would be stretching, and Marcel would just sit and get dressed. And we sat next to each other in the locker room in L.A., so it was before a game, and he just kind of got up, and he bent down twice and barely touched his toes. And then he looked at me with a little smile and goes, 'That's it, I'm ready!' That was his stretching. I couldn't believe it. I just started to laugh, I thought it was the funniest thing.

"I also remember in those days that there were no clickers for the TV. So, when we were roommates on the road, because I was the youngest, I always had to go and turn the TV off. And he'd get mad at me because I would always fall asleep before him."

Beyond providing his roommate with curious bits of humour, Dionne can be credited for setting an example that Robitaille would follow in the Kings' new era and throughout his career. "Marcel was the oldest man I knew, and I was looking at him like a dad. But to see his passion for the game, to see how much he wanted to play every night, and how much he still loved it, that really amazed me. When you come into the league as a young player you have all this passion, and you don't think an older veteran thinks like you, or sees the game like you. Well, Marcel's passion for the game, and winning, was amazing.

"I think Marcel went through every season wanting to win, wanting to be in the playoffs. People don't know that about him because he was a quiet leader, and his way to get prepared for the game was to be quiet. And to a certain degree, over the years, I think Marcel was misunderstood by some of the players that played with him. When I would be driving to the games with him, all he would talk about was how excited he was to be playing that night. He'd say that he couldn't wait, and that it was a big game to win, and we had to win because we wanted to get into the playoffs. I mean, he would talk about it constantly. And the minute he entered the locker room, his way to get focused for a game was to be very serious. That was his way. But I think a lot of players never saw the other side of Marcel—how excited he was to go to the game, and how much he loved the game. I think some of the players had the impression that he was so serious that it was almost just a business for him. And yet, the only reason this guy played all those years was because he loved it so much. I couldn't believe it. He was excited every single game we played that year. And I was shocked by that."

While the NHL was, and remains, a business, and Dionne certainly treated it as such, another relevant truth was his unfaltering will to succeed in that business. And what was required for that success was the passion and desire that Robitaille had witnessed in the latter stage of Dionne's career. By his sixteenth NHL season, time was no longer on Marcel's side, and his goal of competing for the Stanley Cup was becoming a fading dream. He could also see the writing on the wall. With the success of rookie forwards Luc Robitaille and Jimmy Carson, Dionne would receive less and less ice time the following year. As the midway point of the season—and, more importantly for Dionne, the trade deadline—approached, Marcel contacted his general manager, Rogie Vachon, to address his future.

"When I came back to the Kings our team was pretty weak, really," Vachon reflects. "I remember that first year I was GM; at the end of the season I let go of twenty-one players in the organization—some players on our team, some in the minor leagues and some of the players I didn't re-sign. We really didn't have any depth. So we had to rebuild from scratch and it was a very difficult time.

"Jerry Buss was the owner then, and we sort of had a five-year plan. We talked about it and decided that that was the only way to get better, to try to make changes. Then I went out and got Pat Quinn as a coach. And to this day, Pat is still a great coach, one of the greatest motivators you'll ever find. Wherever he goes he's always been successful. He commands a lot of respect; he's big and strong and mean—and very smart. He always had a good system and players played for him.

"All of a sudden we have Luc Robitaille, Steve Duchesne and Jimmy Carson, and these guys started to come around. We really started to have a decent team, and Marcel was part of the plan. But Marcel was getting to the end of his career, and actually, I was the one that traded Marcel when I was the general manager there. It was a very difficult thing to do, but sometimes when you're the GM you've got to do things that are not always pleasant.

"I think what happened was Pat came to me and he was saying that Marcel was getting to the end of his career and he wanted to phase him out a little bit. You know, start playing the kids a little more and keep Marcel for special teams, especially the power play. Superstars in general don't accept that very well. They're used to being in the spotlight all of the time, they're used to being *the* man. And then, when you sort of push them back a little bit, they don't like it. And Marcel was no exception. I could see that he was not very happy, and then the day before the [trade] deadline he called me in the office. We started talking, and he said, 'Listen, I like what you guys are doing here,' because he liked the kids. He really took two of them under his wing—Robitaille and Duchesne, if I remember correctly—because they were very young so he had them living at his place. And he had a very nice influence on those two kids. But we started talking, and he said, 'Well, we're not close to winning the Cup here—I like the things that you guys are doing, but if you could find me a place where I'd have a chance to win the Cup, I wouldn't mind going somewhere else.'

"So I only had, like, twenty-four hours to see if I could work a trade. I wound up trading him to the New York Rangers. They needed a guy like Marcel, especially on the power play. And at that time they were a much stronger team than we were. He still didn't win the Cup, but at least he had a better chance."

"I had been traded to Boston," Charlie Simmer says, "and I remember reading about some problems Marcel was having in L.A. Rogie was still the general manager then, and the next thing you know he was traded to New York. We played them the next day and we talked a little bit in the hallway, and it was just a matter of, well, it can happen to anybody. I think he was happy to be traded to New York, yet I think he was very upset that after all those years that's what happened to him. I think it was a double-edged sword. Even though L.A. was not the hockey mecca of the world, it was Marcel Dionne. L.A. was Marcel Dionne, and it was over."

Long before the trade, there were issues that led up to, and quite likely played a deciding role in, Dionne's departure. Aside from the whole lax approach that Dionne had contested for years, he sincerely felt that the Kings could compete in the L.A. sports marketplace, which had been dominated for years by the successful Lakers. Nevertheless, in Dionne's mind the organization fell short of exploiting the team's marketing potential, which ultimately hindered the franchise. In this regard, Dionne simply had a higher standard that the organization failed to meet. And although such issues were not open for discussion, Marcel was disappointed.

When he looks back on the possibility of staying in L.A., which could have served both parties well in the long run, the communication that might have enabled Dionne to take on more of a supportive role, rather than just being phased out, never took place. "I could see where the team was going and I thought, 'Give me a chance to think about this. If I'm put in a situation where you don't want to use me as much, well, you have to protect me.' I don't want the press to come and question me if I'm not playing as much as I normally would in order to help the young players. A lot of times teams don't do that. They did it with Dale Hunter, but with me they just thought, 'Jesus, we can't talk to him.' They never addressed anything; they never talked to me.

"I had a lot of anger in me, because things were never done right. Every time they made a trade it was just for the sake of making a trade. We had Ray Bourque. We had him in the draft, and they gave it away. You look at these things and it makes you angry."

The trade Dionne mentions was made in October 1978. In search of a goaltender to replace the departed Rogie Vachon, the Kings traded their first-round pick in the 1979 draft to Boston for Ron Grahame. Grahame never became the starter in L.A., and two years later was sold to the Quebec Nordiques. With L.A.'s pick, the Bruins drafted Bourque, who played for twenty-two seasons and was a five-time winner of the Norris Trophy as the NHL's best defenceman.

The transaction that ended Marcel's tenure as a King was, similarly, a head-scratcher. In recent years, a sort of ritual has evolved around the NHL's March trading deadline, in which weaker teams parcel up their veterans and ship them off to contenders. The departing player usually gets a chance at a Stanley Cup, while his former team hopes to get players or draft picks that will be useful further down the road. The Dionne deal doesn't fit this profile. The trade—Dionne, minor-leaguer Jeff Crossman and a third-round draft pick to New York for veterans Bob Carpenter and Tom Laidlaw—did little to improve the Kings. Even though it was initiated at the eleventh hour, and at the player's urging, Los Angeles failed to get value for its signature player, who was still producing at a point-a-game clip. According to Tiger Williams, the trade was symptomatic of the way the Kings consistently undervalued Dionne.

"There have been certain players on certain teams over the years—whether it's Yzerman in Detroit or Lafleur in Montreal or Bobby Orr in Boston, every team had a guy—and Marcel was the guy in L.A. As far as I was concerned, he never got put on the pedestal enough and wasn't high enough above everybody else. I'd been in the league for fourteen years and I'd already been on four teams, so I kind of knew what was going on in the league. And the people in L.A., mostly in the management area . . . they just didn't get it. I mean, most teams would dream of—they'd be doing backflips if they had a guy like Dionne that they could hook their advertising and everything around. And they never took advantage of that.

"At the time, I kind of encouraged Marcel to go. He'd been there a long, long time, for a dozen years—and then, to leave, it's tough. But I told him he might play another five or six years if he goes somewhere else.

"When management gets it in their heads that they want to change things, whether or not it's for the good, they're going to do it. And you can go around the league and sit down with guys and they'll tell you a whole book full of stories like that. When they decide that they don't want you around, you're done!

"The only reason Marcel got traded out of there was that they were scared of him. He was more powerful than they were. Now, that's strictly my opinion. Then Pat Quinn went to Vancouver, and there was that whole fiasco where he got suspended for a year for signing when he was still under contract. He did what he thought was best for his career and his interests and that's what happened. And what did that do for us in L.A.? Again, there we were in L.A. with the greatest waves for surfing, and no f—king surfboard! That's where I had a lot of compassion for Marcel. He'd been put through that sixteen times, but he still performed on the ice. They never gave him and that nucleus of guys—you know, when they had Charlie [Simmer] before he broke his legs, and Dave Taylor, they had some great players, but they never ever surrounded those guys with strong management and leadership.

"I thought they had some real sad sacks there. I thought they had guys that just didn't get it. They didn't understand what the game was all about, didn't understand what it took to win on a consistent basis. And my own belief is that they wore Marcel down."

Mike Murphy, who was by now the Kings' coach, weighs in with a similar assessment. "I wasn't involved in the trade other than the fact that I was coaching the team at the time. I was called and told, 'This is the deal we're going to make, and what do you think of it?' It didn't matter if I liked it or not; it was going to be done. I was surprised we decided to trade him. And I'm not sure there wasn't a huge void left on the team. Marcel was a kingpin for the fans, an identifiable guy. He was a standup guy. He took criticism and kept on going. And suddenly there wasn't anybody there like that. We hoped at the time it would be a chance for some of the younger players to flourish—and I'm not sure that happened. In fact, I know it *didn't* happen."

Of all the factors that figured in the decision to let Marcel go— his dissatisfaction with the organization, his age amongst a wealth of young talent, or simply a desire on the part of player and management alike for a fresh start—it is difficult to say which carried the most weight. Nevertheless, Rogie Vachon acted upon Dionne's request with little time and good intentions. Close to Marcel all season long, Luc Robitaille was quick to learn of Dionne's fate. "I was in shock. I didn't believe it. He talked to me and he said that he thought he was going to be traded, and later on when he called and told me that the trade had happened, honestly, I really didn't believe it. I mean, he's Mr. L.A. This is the guy that put hockey on the map in L.A. for all of those years. I honestly didn't believe it.

"It's funny because that's how brutal professional sports can be sometimes, to a certain degree. That year, Marcel was the guy that helped Jimmy Carson, Steve Duchesne and myself. And he was so excited to play and to see that the team was revitalized. And that had a lot to do with him—the way he helped us and the way he took care of us.

"But management hadn't talked to him about picking up another year on his contract, so he went to ask them. I can't remember his exact words, but I think he felt that he kind of screwed up. He said to them, 'If you're not going to sign me, you might as well trade me.' But I think he thought that they were going to say, 'No, no.' It wasn't a bluff on Marcel's part, because Marcel isn't a bluffer. But I know deep down, Marcel wanted to stay in L.A. When he said 'Trade me,' he didn't think that they would take him that seriously, that quickly. And they did."

Chapter Twelve

"**I** HAD GONE for a haircut when I got the call from Rogie," recalls Marcel Dionne about the day he was traded to New York. "He said, 'We're working on a deal right now, why don't you come down to the office?' I went down there and he told me he had talked to Phil [Esposito, then the New York Rangers' GM], and they were able to work out a deal. It was an emotional time. After the thing with Pat Quinn going to Vancouver, Mike Murphy became head coach. It was tough because I really liked Mike and I wanted to contribute. But then again, you don't know what they want. So I shook hands with a few people, had tears and I just left.

"When I made the decision to leave, my wife didn't know. And when Carol found out, she wasn't happy. She cried for three months, she was so mad at me. She said, 'You and your big mouth.' And I knew that I was giving up a nice lifestyle for my family. But I had to leave. I had to make the move to get me going, to get focused again, to go on and do something else. New York was not the answer, but it was a way out. So I thought, 'I'll take the way out.'"

If the upside to transplanting his career and family was to better his chances of winning the Stanley Cup, with New York, Dionne didn't improve his chances by much. Nor did he land on a team with more organizational stability. In 1986–87 the Rangers were plagued by coaching difficulties that resulted in general manager Phil Esposito manning the bench for the majority of games. On the ice, the team was inadequate in several areas. Amongst the weak spots was a lack of scoring punch up the middle. Esposito hoped that acquiring Dionne would alleviate that need.

Finishing the season with the Rangers, Dionne contributed 10 points in 14 games. There were no miracles performed in New York that spring, and Dionne had to face a more difficult period of adjustment than he might have imagined. Repeatedly suffering consecutive sleepless nights, Marcel contemplated the position he had created for himself and his family. "Once I got there, then the reality sank in. Tommy Webster was the coach, and he got sick, so Phil coached the rest of the season. They had serious problems in New York. We made it into the playoffs, but lost against the Flyers in the first round."

Dionne was better off in New York than with another team where he might have been a third- or fourth-line centre, but beyond that, there was no great cause for celebration. To the media, he offered his feelings on the trade—in typical fashion, honestly and brutally so. "I spoke with the press after the trade and told them what had happened. I shouldn't have said anything, but what I said was the truth. I told them that I didn't want to get traded. When I said that, it was interpreted as I didn't want to be in New York. But that wasn't true. I was happy to be in New York when I was there. I explained to them that I had gone to Vachon and I gambled on it. I rolled the dice. I called their bluff on whether they really wanted me—and I lost."

In his heart, Dionne was not ready to leave L.A., yet he remained eager to play if there was genuine interest. As far as Dionne knew, despite whatever problems may or may not have existed, he would get to play a regular shift in New York—and that was a step forward.

That summer, the Dionne family bid farewell to its California home, and while Carol and daughter Lisa might have done so reluctantly at the time, hindsight eventually allowed them to see the benefit of the move. "California was a great place," Marcel enthused. "We all liked it. I went to work, and it wasn't bad. The paycheques were good. But some places are better than others in terms of allowing you to raise your kids the right way. You want a place where there are values. In L.A., you couldn't do it. It's a place where money buys your way. But money doesn't buy values. The school there wasn't that great, and the kids all wanted to go to the beach, and it's drugs and drinking and 'who cares?'

"My daughter was devastated when we left California. But years later, when the Kings retired my number, Lisa thanked Rogie Vachon. She said, 'I want to thank you very much. You trading my dad was the best thing that ever happened to my family and me.' She found a new life in New York and discovered that leaving California wasn't such a bad thing."

The hiring of head coach Michel Bergeron for the 1987–88 season settled the Rangers' coaching dilemma. Bergeron, a feisty French-Canadian, had decent success with the Quebec Nordiques through the peak of the Michel Goulet–Stastny Brothers era. However, in his New York debut, without a team as deep in talent as his Nordiques roster, Bergeron would miss the playoffs for the first time in eight seasons of coaching in the NHL. For Dionne, the postseason disappointment was all too familiar.

The Rangers' top three scorers that season were Walt Poddubny (38 goals, 50 assists), Kelly Kisio (23 goals, 55 assists) and Tomas Sandstrom (28 goals, 40 assists). Dionne's tally of 31 goals and 34 assists in 67 games placed him just a shade behind Sandstrom in points and second only to Poddubny in goals. At the very least, Dionne had proven his worth. As it was, Marcel was in the position to provide solid support, but without a nucleus of quality players and one or two legitimate stars, real success wasn't about to happen anytime soon.

Bergeron found the demand for better results in New York was immediate and pressing. Unable to produce a winning team overnight, he took another approach. In a move that not only won the favour of New York fans, but also gained the attention of the entire hockey world, he shrewdly brokered the return of one of the highest-profile players in the history of the game. Out of retirement, suiting up for the Rangers the following season, was none other than Guy Lafleur.

The hype surrounding Lafleur's return to action was incredible.

After an awkward split from the Canadiens organization the ever-popular Flower had been out of hockey for more than three seasons, but he remained in tremendous shape. For the Manhattan hopeful, the pairing of Dionne and Lafleur, two Hall of Famers with a shared history that dated back twenty years, had the makings of a storybook ending.

What did transpire were flashes of brilliance that the old Lafleur fans enjoyed on the occasional highlight reel. There was also a triumphant return to the Montreal Forum, at which the chant of "Guy, Guy, Guy" echoed all night long. But with injury abbreviating his comeback season to 67 games, Lafleur was held to 18 goals and 27 assists. Although his return to hockey gave the Rangers a publicity boost, Lafleur's New York tenure ended that season. After two perfunctory seasons with the Quebec Nordiques, the vaunted comeback was over, a brief footnote to a truly great career.

While Bergeron received laurels for engineering the Lafleur comeback, and Lafleur enjoyed the limelight, Marcel Dionne was unceremoniously shifted to the back burner. Although his conditioning might have been subpar at the very outset of the year, that shouldn't have been news for anyone—or cause for concern. After an effective first season with the Rangers, Dionne was simply discarded. It was a decision that infuriated those who cared for Marcel.

"Michel Bergeron is a funny guy. When Marcel was in New York, Bergeron called Guy Lafleur to bring him there, which is fine, to want to have Guy Lafleur," says Rénald Dionne. "But the year before, Marcel scored 31 goals. So he brought in Lafleur and took Marcel out, pushed him aside to give Lafleur more ice time. And Lafleur scored 18 goals that year. How can you push aside a guy who scored 31 goals to make room for a guy who scored 18? Well, he wanted to please the people of Quebec. And Bergeron was smart, because in Quebec he was treated like a god. But it wasn't right, what he did to Marcel."

That season, the Dionne family, who attended every game

Marcel played in Montreal, experienced just how unsympathetic life in the NHL could be. After a career spent dazzling fans throughout the league, and having played some of his best games in Montreal, Marcel was benched specifically for a game at the Forum, yet was told he would play the next game in Quebec City. Carol Dionne seethes, "Do you know how much it hurt the family to be there to watch?!"

Rather than take issue with management over his benching, Dionne held himself accountable for his own performance—or lack thereof. Marcel knew that he was not in game shape, and whether that was a result of his diminished playing time or the cause of it became irrelevant. In Marcel's mind, he was out of the lineup and the situation had to be rectified.

It happened that Dionne's old friend Peter Mahovlich was coaching the Rangers' farm team in Denver. Dionne wanted to play his way back into shape, and with no inflated ego to get in his way, Marcel picked up the phone.

"I was surprised when he called," Mahovlich remembers, "because I didn't think the top of the organization would want him to go down to the minors. And I didn't think they'd be willing to let him go down. When he explained what he had in mind, basically, I said to him, 'I think it's great.' If you want to prove to yourself that you're able to play and you want to be in the best shape possible, play five or six games at the minor level and then go back to a good situation. I thought he had the right idea.

"The fact that he was willing to do that—after that career? It tells you an awful lot about what kind of person Marcel is. He didn't feel that he was finished and he didn't want to just sit there and collect his money. He wanted to *earn* his money. That's what it tells you about Marcel."

And so the curious footnote at the end of Marcel Dionne's career is a stint of nine games with the Denver Rangers of the International Hockey League, during which he assisted on thirteen goals. But there would be no reward from the Rangers for his humility and effort in the minors; they had begun the process of overhauling the team and organization. Michel Bergeron, who years later would apologize to Dionne for his regrettable treatment of him, was fired with two games remaining on the regular-season schedule. In the first round of the playoffs, the Pittsburgh Penguins defeated the Rangers in four straight games. Marcel Dionne did not play.

In the 1988–89 season, Dionne's last in the NHL, he was cut back to a scattered 37 games in which he mustered 7 goals and 16 assists. His legs were not moving as they used to, and the weight they carried had become a heavier load. Despite his will to compete, Marcel Dionne's career in professional hockey had come to an end.

With no ties to the game dictating their next move, Marcel and Carol were now free to settle down where they pleased. However, the decision of where to sink their roots would take a few years to iron out. Although they had spent the majority of their adult life in California, returning to the west coast was never a consideration. After a brief stay outside New York City, Dionne wanted to find a community that would better suit his family's needs. Eventually, they would settle in a suburb of Buffalo, New York. Being close to Carol's home of St. Catharines, Ontario, while residing in the agreeable state of New York, the family was offered the best of both worlds. Now more so than ever, Marcel was able to enjoy his time doing what meant most to him away from the rink.

"He spent all of his free time with his wife and kids," says Luc Robitaille. "He was awesome that way. He's also a very smart individual. He knew a lot about real estate and different things. So he was very smart off the ice, but the majority of his time was always spent with his family."

Bound by the demands of a hectic schedule, Marcel, like all professional athletes, had spent a good part of the year separated from his wife and kids. Nonetheless, he is extremely proud of his enduring marriage and has always been a dependable parent. Whatever generalizations might be made about people in high-profile careers, Dionne assures that all caring families have the same concerns and face the same difficulties when it comes to raising their children. As far as the pressure of growing up with celebrity, and a parent that is often away, are concerned, Dionne is reluctant to accept these as justification for a crutch.

"I think it's all bullshit, to always say that the dad was never there," he says. "You know what? The thing is, the dad has to make sure he's there when it's *time* to be there. I look at my mom and dad. My dad worked from nine to five for all of his life. And he has been with my mom for every day of his life since they've been married. He's never even been away for a week. I couldn't live with my wife like that, and she couldn't live with me like that—but that's all right. You need your space. And my parents manage and they adjust. We all have our different ways of making it work.

"On television, you see families that are too good to be true, like they're perfect. I say, 'Great, but is that really fun—to be perfect?' You have to have crisis. As long as your kids know right from wrong. And that's what I tell Carol. It's okay to challenge our kids; they have to figure things out. So sometimes they tell you to f— off—so what? They figure it out and they come around.

"I've also seen kids that are just lost. They haven't received the love, and that's tough. I see that a lot with the kids of divorced parents—they're troubled and they rebel. Now, I'm not a psychologist, but I think to say that it's just about love is overrated. It's not so much about love as it is about understanding. We say love—I love you, or I need love. I need a hug. Well, sure, that's fine, that's part of it. But more than that, I believe kids need understanding. If a kid strays off course, and they get back on track, what they need is understanding of what they are going through. With understanding, everything else will fall into place. Love will fall into place."

Since his retirement from hockey, Dionne has explored a number of ventures, ranging from a dry-cleaning business to a spell working with young talent in the L.A. Kings organization. Not surprisingly, he has found his niche running a successful family business that bears his name, Marcel Dionne Enterprises. On any given day, Marcel can be found in his impressive retail store working alongside his daughter Lisa. Along with other interests in developing properties and building homes, the various activities of Marcel Dionne Enterprises allow him to keep up with old friends.

Steve Shutt speaks highly of Marcel's commitment to his old friends. "Marcel is one of the very, very few players, or former players, that cares enough to do something for another former player. A lot of guys say they are going to do something, but they don't. You know, to help this guy or help that guy. Whenever you see Marcel at a golf tournament, a speaking engagement or something like that, he's always got somebody with him. And it's always somebody that, if it wasn't for Marcel, this guy wouldn't have been a guest speaker, or wouldn't have been at the golf tournament. Marcel has certainly helped a lot of players doing stuff like that."

While many wonderful things have come to the Dionne family as a result of Marcel's career, he has always been generous in embracing opportunities to give back to the community. For reasons close to home, Marcel has spent a great deal of time working with charities and people fighting illness. Today he has a keen understanding of how people can help. "I've learned through hockey, spending time with handicapped children or terminally ill people, that they don't want people to feel sorry for them. They know where they're at. You have to talk to them—ask them the direct question. If you ask the right question, they're going to give you an answer, and they're going to feel good about it.

"I feel that I am blessed, so I'm happy to help out where I can. Sometimes I'll be at a health-related benefit and people will point out that I don't have to be there. I'll tell them to shut up, I'm happy to be there. And I talk to these people and listen to what they have to say, and I encourage them to learn and research about their illness. I'll ask them if they are getting the best treatment possible. And people appreciate that directness.

"You can't meet every request, but I do as much as I can. I have been involved with colitis and Crohn's disease for twenty years. My son-in-law has it, and I try to make sure he is doing all he can to help himself with diet, staying in shape, and so on. And if he has to have an operation down the road, it's a plumbing job. That's all it is. Thousands of people have it done and they live with it. So you have to try to control the disease versus letting it control you.

"A lot of people don't understand that they have a good life, and that they should be happy. Sure we all have to better ourselves. But it's not necessarily wealth. We all want money—but if you have your health, and you have a good relationship, then you've won the battle. That's what life is about."

Beyond his day-to-day life with Carol, Lisa, Garrett and Drew, Marcel has kept up healthy relationships with his own siblings. While all of his sisters and brothers have succeeded in their own fields, several profess that it wasn't always easy to be related to a superstar. Strong in character, Marcel's sisters often resented the assumption that items they earned on their own were gifts from their brother. Sister Lorraine asserts, "We were very happy for Marcel, but sometimes it was difficult. Like, if somebody in the family bought a new car, people would say, 'Did Marcel give that to you?' And some of these people [jumping to conclusions] were family—aunts and uncles! But we were very happy when he would visit us back when he was playing. And we would all be waiting on him, 'Do you want a coffee? Can I get you a beer, Marcel?'" Lorraine chuckles. "Now he can get it himself."

Perhaps the most challenging relationship Marcel had with any of his siblings was with his brother Gilbert Jr., who is nineteen years younger than him. When Gilbert embarked on his own pro career, it was Marcel's hope that his younger brother would avoid some of the hazards he ran into. While Gilbert is now grateful for how his brother tried to help him, not everything panned out as well as the young Dionne would have liked.

"Because of our age difference, we really didn't have a close brotherly relationship," Gilbert says. "And as I was starting my hockey career, Marcel was trying to make sure that I was on the right track. Back then, I was thinking, 'I don't need him to tell me what's what. I want him as a brother, not a dad.'

"One thing he did do that was great, he made sure I was living with a good family when I was playing junior in Niagara Falls. He assured our parents that I would be well looked after and under control. When you're fifteen and sixteen you don't know what's happening. You have no worries, no responsibilities . . . you play hockey and go to school and that's it. So he made sure that behind the scenes I was staying in line, living with a good family. I stayed with a good friend of his, Al Boone, and sure enough Al's son married Marcel's daughter."

As fate would have it, the Montreal Canadiens, who in the 1971 draft passed over Marcel in favour of Guy Lafleur, drafted Gilbert Dionne. For Gilbert, while it was an honour to play for the Canadiens, with it came the burden of the competitive press in Montreal. Unfortunately for the younger Dionne, he was perhaps a little too outspoken for his own good. "I've said things that I shouldn't have said things. . . . You learn by your mistakes. But I love Montreal; I wish I were still there. Looking back, with ten years under my belt, I would have dealt with it differently. And I think that if I had been closer to Marcel, maybe he could have guided me that way."

Although the younger Dionne's time in the NHL was brief, he certainly made the most of it. In the playoffs after his second year with the Habs, Gilbert netted six goals to go with six assists, and in so doing helped the Montreal Canadiens win the Stanley Cup in 1993. Of much greater significance was the joy that Gilbert brought to his family—at long last, the family name of Dionne had made it onto the Stanley Cup.

"I remember I was in Los Angeles on business during the finals, and I flew back to Montreal to be there for the last game," Marcel recalls. "And it was Serge Savard who came through and got me two tickets. I was so proud of the Montreal Canadiens. I walked in there and they treated me great. After they won, they welcomed me into the dressing room—and I got my picture taken with Gilbert and the Cup.

"People say to me, 'It's a shame that you never won the Stanley Cup,' and of course I wanted to win it. But there was no better or bigger thrill for me than to see my brother play in the NHL and win the Cup. That was the ultimate. I remember the night they won; we stayed in Montreal and I drove to Drummondville the next day. I pulled into my parents' driveway and my dad came out and gave me a big hug and said, 'We finally won the Cup.' That was great.'"

"I think Marcel always had a burning desire to win," Dave Taylor says. "You know, I've played with Wayne Gretzky and some top-notch players, and Marcel Dionne belongs in that class. What I came to appreciate about Marcel, after having played for a number of years myself, is that when you made a play and passed him the puck, he had the ability to finish. And that's always nice, because you play with other players and you can make plays and give them an opportunity and the puck doesn't go in the net. But it was an absolute pleasure to play alongside Marcel, with the intensity that he brought to the game.

"Everybody talks about the significance of Wayne Gretzky coming to L.A. And that was tremendously significant. I mean, it really lifted the profile of hockey, not just in Los Angeles, but throughout the United States. And I've said a number of times, I don't think we'd have a team in Anaheim, in San Jose, in Dallas, in Florida, or in Tampa Bay if Gretzky hadn't come to L.A. But at the same time, I'm not sure we'd have hockey in L.A. today if we didn't have Marcel Dionne. In that era, Marcel Dionne *was* the Los Angeles Kings."

At the time of his retirement from hockey, only Gordie Howe and Wayne Gretzky had scored more points than Marcel Dionne. Now with each passing year, a few players have chipped away at Dionne's totals. And a few more might pass him yet, as Mark Messier and Ron Francis have recently done. Nevertheless, the standard Dionne set for those who followed was remarkable. His exceptional talents sustained the direction and vision the NHL had for its future. Of his eighteen years in the NHL, twelve were spent, in his prime, carrying a team and nourishing a sport in a non-traditional market. The NHL has built on that success ever since, thanks in part to the first great player of the modern era— Marcel Dionne.

Acknowledgments

FOR their kindness and support, I would like to thank the Dionne family—Marcel's lovely wife, Carol, and their children, Lisa, Garrett and Drew; Marcel's parents, Gilbert and Laurette; and his siblings, Rénald, Linda, Guylaine, Lorraine, Chantal, Marlène and Gilbert Jr.

Thanks to the following people for their generosity in contributing to this book: Bill Bird, Jack Gatecliff, Marvin Goldblatt, Glenn Goldup, George Hulme, Dave Hutchison, Dick Irvin, Nick Libett, Peter Mahovlich, Brian McKenzie, Bob Miller, Mike Murphy, Gilbert Perreault, Mickey Redmond, Luc Robitaille, Steve Shutt, Charlie Simmer, Dave Taylor, Skeeter Teal, Rogie Vachon, Bryan Watson and Dave Williams.

To the staff at HarperCollins, thank you for your help and expertise.

For their enthusiastic assistance, I would like to thank Craig Campbell (and the Hockey Hall of Fame Archives), hockeydb.com, Paul Patskou and Lloyd Davis.

To Ron MacLean, I offer my sincere gratitude for writing a wonderful foreword.

A special thank you must go to Leanne Johnson—for everything, and to David Matheson, who does an outstanding job of looking out for me. Thanks so much.

To my family—Margaret, Mom, Dad, Michael, Nancy, Auntie Anne, Uncle Peter and the rest of the tree—my thanks and love.

Lastly, I would like to thank Marcel for the opportunity to write this book, for being a great person and for being patient throughout. Thanks, Marce.

DIONNE, MARCEL C–R. 5′7″, 185 lbs.   B: Drummondville, Que, 8/3/1951.
Detroit's 1st choice, 2nd overall, in 1971 Amateur Draft.

			REGULAR SEASON				PLAYOFFS							
Season	Club	League	GP	G	A	Pts	GP	G	A	Pts	PIM	PP	SH	GW
1968–69	St. Catharines Black Hawks	OHA	48	37	63	100	…	…	…	…	…	…	…	…
1969–70	St. Catharines Black Hawks	OHA	54	55	77	132	…	…	…	…	…	…	…	…
1970–71	St. Catharines Black Hawks	OHA	46	62	81	143	…	…	…	…	…	…	…	…
1971–72	Detroit Red Wings	NHL	78	28	49	77	…	…	…	…	…	…	…	…
1972–73	Canada	Summit	DID NOT PLAY				…	…	…	…	…	…	…	…
	Detroit Red Wings	NHL	77	40	50	90	…	…	…	…	…	…	…	…
1973–74	Detroit Red Wings	NHL	74	24	54	78	…	…	…	…	…	…	…	…
1974–75	Detroit Red Wings	NHL	80	47	74	121	…	…	…	…	…	…	…	…
1975–76	Los Angeles Kings	NHL	80	40	54	94	9	6	1	7	0	3	0	0
1976–77	Canada	C Cup	7	1	5	6	…	…	…	…	…	…	…	…
	Los Angeles Kings	NHL	80	53	69	122	9	5	9	14	2	1	0	1
1977–78	Los Angeles Kings	NHL	70	36	43	79	2	0	0	0	0	0	0	0
	Canada	WEC-A	10	9	3	12	…	…	…	…	…	…	…	…
1978–79	Los Angeles Kings	NHL	80	59	71	130	2	0	1	1	1	0	0	0
	NHL All-Stars	Chal Cup	2	0	1	1	…	…	…	…	…	…	…	…
	Canada	WEC-A	7	2	1	3	…	…	…	…	…	…	…	…
1979–80	Los Angeles Kings	NHL	80	53	84	137	4	0	3	3	4	0	0	0
1980–81	Los Angeles Kings	NHL	80	58	77	135	4	1	3	4	7	1	0	0
1981–82	Canada	C Cup	6	4	1	5	…	…	…	…	…	…	…	…
	Los Angeles Kings	NHL	78	50	67	117	10	7	4	11	0	4	0	0
1982–83	Los Angeles Kings	NHL	80	56	51	107	…	…	…	…	…	…	…	…
	Canada	WEC-A	10	6	3	9	…	…	…	…	…	…	…	…
1983–84	Los Angeles Kings	NHL	66	39	53	92	…	…	…	…	…	…	…	…
1984–85	Los Angeles Kings	NHL	80	46	80	126	3	1	2	3	2	1	0	0
1985–86	Los Angeles Kings	NHL	80	36	58	94	…	…	…	…	…	…	…	…
	Canada	WEC-A	10	4	4	8	…	…	…	…	…	…	…	…
1986–87	Los Angeles Kings	NHL	67	24	50	74	…	…	…	…	…	…	…	…
	New York Rangers	NHL	14	4	6	10	6	1	1	2	2	1	0	0

			REGULAR SEASON				PLAYOFFS							
Season	Club	League	GP	G	A	Pts	GP	G	A	Pts	PIM	PP	SH	GW
1987–88	New York Rangers	NHL	67	31	34	65	...	...	...	...	...	...	...	...
1988–89	New York Rangers	NHL	37	7	16	23	...	...	...	...	...	...	...	...
	Denver Rangers	IHL	9	0	13	13	...	...	...	...	...	...	...	...
	NHL Totals		1348	731	1040	1771	49	21	24	45	17	11	0	1

OHA Second All-Star Team (1970) • OHA First All-Star Team (1971) • Won Lady Byng Trophy (1975, 1977) • NHL First All-Star Team (1977, 1980) • Named Best Forward at WEC-A (1978) • NHL Second All-Star Team (1979, 1981) • Won Lester B. Pearson Award (1979, 1980) • Won Art Ross Trophy (1980)

Played in NHL All-Star Game (1975,1976,1977, 1978,1980, 1981, 1983, 1985)

Rights traded to LA Kings by Detroit with Bart Crashley for Terry Harper, Dan Maloney and LA Kings 2nd round choice (later traded to Minnesota—Minnesota selected Jim Roberts) in 1976 Amateur Draft, June 23, 1975. Traded to NY Rangers by LA Kings with Jeff Crossman and LA Kings' 3rd round choice in 1989 Entry Draft (later traded to Minnesota—Minnesota selected Murray Garbutt) in 1989 Entry Draft for Bob Carpenter and Tom Laidlaw, March 10, 1987.

GP Games played • **G** Goals scored • **A** Assists • **Pts** Points • **PIM** Penalties in minutes • **PP** Power play goals • **SH** Shorthanded goals • **GW** Game-winning goals

Index

Index